T0194820

WINNING WITH THE FRIEND WITHIN

*A Nurse's Journey of Hope and
Five Essentials to Help Heal
A Hurting World*

Monica R. Pierre

BALBOA.PRESS
A DIVISION OF HAY HOUSE

Balboa Press books may be ordered through booksellers or by contacting:

Balboa Press
A Division of Hay House
1663 Liberty Drive
Bloomington, IN 47403
www.balboapress.com
844-682-1282

Scripture quotations are from the Holy Bible, King James Version (Authorized Version). First published in 1611. Quoted from the KJV Classic Reference Bible, Copyright © 1983 by The Zondervan Corporation.

ISBN: 979-8-7652-4225-4 (sc)
ISBN: 979-8-7652-4227-8 (hc)
ISBN: 979-8-7652-4226-1 (e)

Library of Congress Control Number: 2023909132

Balboa Press rev. date: 07/14/2023

To my high school French and English teacher
Leroy C. G. Wesley II
(1944–2016)

Mr. Wesley,
Thank you for introducing the right tools
and *friend* to help me win.

I have stood on a mountain of no's for one yes.

—B. Smith

CONTENTS

PART THREE: YOUR WAYS (ACTIONS): WHATEVER YOU PUT OUT COMES BACK

PART FOUR: YOUR WISDOM (INSIGHT): YOUR PLATFORM IS ON DIVINE DISPLAY

PART FIVE: YOUR WIN (YOUR WORLD): BE THE RISING TIDE

PREFACE

From childhood to adulthood, we must do a lot of deconditioning. Somewhere between the time we are born and the moment we can speak our very first words, the innocence of our true nature is totally disrupted.

We receive verbal and nonverbal cues from everything around us. From our family customs and religious beliefs to our socioeconomic status and educational background, we adopt a certain mindset.

Until life gives us further notice, we often find ourselves on society's hectic schedule, competing with and comparing ourselves to one another until things get too complicated. We then either patch ourselves up for further turmoil, or we collapse and finally surrender to the place and *power* from which it all started. Unless we do this, we continue to suffer and eventually die—figuratively, that is.

But there is hope. There is still an ongoing and sweet possibility to win.

Winning is not determined by the demographics of where we live, our line of work, our titles, our degrees, how much money we have, or who our family, friends, and connections are—or the lack thereof. Winning is the awareness and application of our divinely inherited worth, which cannot be defined by the world. Therefore, it cannot be exchanged, and there is no such equal value on the planet. There is a victory we receive and have access to from the moment we are created. Society's view can lead us to think that our true worth is determined by our material possessions or how close we are to the spotlight. This drives the false reality that if it looks good and appears well put together on the surface, then it really is. That is not necessarily true. What is real is that which resides within us.

In this book, I share my tried-and-true experiences and describe the only constant source you can lean on in this life. I truly believe that when we are well and whole from within, nothing can shatter us from without.

This offering was written from a place of unconditional love. It is an invitation to all who are drawn to it, and it is my intention that you are uplifted by it.

Wishing you the greatest love of all,

Monica R. Pierre
Oakland, California

INTRODUCTION

If the Creator had a question, it was never *how* ... but more so *what* and *why*. Everything that exists had an intention from the beginning from the mind of its maker. A man, a woman, and the creation of child is a miracle if nothing else—but there *is* something else. No matter the path, the human existence of everyone who made it out of spirit into flesh came with divine purpose.

On a cold winter morning at 6:45 a.m., a young teenage girl lay anxiously in the labor room with her feet up in stirrups. Uncertain of what life would be, having had just a glimpse of her real self, one thing was for sure. She was about to embark upon a serious unfolding. She was about to be a mother, a very single mother.

Falling in love in her teens had brought her to an unexpected place, which soon became a very lonely one after giving of herself to a young but seemingly trusting courtship. Pregnant at her high school graduation, she journeyed across the stage, not yet knowing if she was carrying a boy or girl. This task alone took up such mental space that the slight consideration of anything more was seemingly impossible. Yet she remained strong and dared herself to become weak. It would be the beginning of an early adulthood and a lonesome struggle. That teen was my mother.

My father arrived at the hospital to get a first look of his infant daughter. "She looks just like me," he said. A few days later, my mother was discharged from the hospital with me. She and I returned home to live with my grandmother. Soon after, in my early years, my father decided to flee. As for me, this was the beginning.

My mother raised me single-handedly. She worked full time and took additional part-time jobs to provide for us. She managed a lot with very little and did everything possible to not let me know how difficult things really were. My maternal grandmother and great-grandma looked after me when my mother was at work.

My father unfortunately remained absent over the years, both physically and supportively. I knew him by face and name, but the relationship, love, and trust were never established. From time to time, he would do a pop-up visit. For the most part, though, as a young man and well into his adult life, he served time in prison off and on for various charges that included drug use, assault and battery, robbery, and theft.

Nonetheless, the story of my life began there. I would have my introduction to this world as a very humble child with no siblings, in a young, single-parent home, within the low-income Martin Luther King Jr. district of my hometown city of Shreveport, Louisiana.

I wish I could tell you that becoming a nurse was my first love, or that it was a part of my childhood dream or discovery. The truth is—based on the way that I grew up and the experiences of lack and limitations within my community—needing a sense of security is what inspired me to go to college and choose a field that could provide it. I needed a key to a better life. I needed the peace in knowing that once I graduated, I could immediately find a job, have a good income, and provide well for myself.

But from a very young age, I was attracted to books and words before I even understood what literature was. I found myself drawn to any tool that would allow me to scribble. Whether with crayons, chalk, pencils, or markers, I would often find something to scribble on. As a little girl, I was fascinated by the extra-large, bright yellow or white, well-known telephone directories, commonly called "telephone books." They were found in most households before there were cell phones and Google. The books were free and published by the phone company, and they were used to search local phone numbers and addresses. It was the largest book in the house, and a new volume was delivered by the mailman periodically. I'd always find my way to its fresh, thin, crisp pages. And yes, to my delight (and my grandmother's upset)—I'd scribble all over it.

I didn't understand it at the time, but I now know that I was in a place of discovering what would become a passion for the written word. This passion would trickle over into many classroom settings, throughout grade school, college, and eventually into my nursing career. I was in an advanced English class in high school, and because I did so well, I was able to graduate a semester early during my senior year and start college.

During nursing school, a commonly known and dreaded assignment is the completion of a "care plan," which involves the process of writing up the anticipated nursing care for each patient based on their symptoms. While care-plan assignments are already lengthy, mine became extra long, because I wanted to tell the entire story about my patients and how they got there. My nursing instructors criticized my super lengthy documentation and complained that it was totally unnecessary for me to write an entire story about my patients based on the information they had shared during my initial assessments. Beyond vital signs, symptoms, and baseline medical data, I'd proceed about what had occurred right before they arrived, including their thoughts, feelings, who was present, and what triggered the events leading to their admission to the hospital. I'd describe their facial expressions, what they were wearing, and gave a full narrative of their tones, sighs, and fears, with appropriate punctuation marks throughout. I could not turn off this drive to write. I treated my patient assessments like an interview and my ongoing care of them like a developing story. How nerve-racking this was for nurses who followed me! Some appreciated these care plans, but they annoyed many. Those who enjoyed it most were my patients. Not only would I take the time to listen and document their journey, but while caring for them I'd also try to dig deeper and find out what was going on internally, emotionally. By the end of their hospital stay, many expressed how they felt so thoroughly and uniquely cared for.

There is a well-known phrase in health care: *"If it's not documented, it wasn't done."* I suppose I did not have an issue with that. I had the most concerns when there were things happening beyond my control, which led me to go deeper within.

One of the things I am certain of is that there is always a root cause that shows up in the form of a symptom. If only the symptoms are treated, the core problem is not resolved.

As a society, we have a multitude of "symptoms" from preexisting conditions that can make the world seem like a sick and ugly place. It is only when we get to the root cause that lies within each of us are we able to start the journey of healing and experience the true beauty of life that exists all around us.

In this book, I will present many insights gained during my most private, spiritual-heart moments. On a deeply personal note, this work is twofold. First, I am now starting to live my truth as a writer. One of the gifts that has always tried to express itself is now pleasing my soul. Second, the healer and empath within me serves in greater ways than the traditional means. I hope that my two worlds blended can bring great inspiration to yours. This world is waiting, and winning begins with *you.*

PART ONE

YOUR WORTH
(BIRTHRIGHT)

YOU ARE WORTHY, AND
EVERYONE ELSE IS TOO

CHAPTER 1

YOU ARE GOD'S BRIGHT IDEA

"Before I formed you in the womb, I knew you."

—JEREMIAH 1:5

T he most freeing thought is that the power that allows the Earth to perfectly rotate around the sun is the same power that causes your heart to beat, your lungs to breathe, and your eyes to blink without you even having to think about it. There are many wonderful names to describe this power—I will start by calling it God.

No matter what has happened to you or what is going on in this world, there is something you must hold fast to. Before the beginning of time, you were an original idea straight from the mind of God, not of your parents and not of society. Your very existence for being on the planet at this specific time was well intended by the Creator.

I know there are many challenges in this life that can lead you to think that you have no purpose or value, but I invite you to go on a journey with me. Think about how you got here. Reflect on your parents and how they met. For some this might be a beautiful love story, for others this might trigger some very uncomfortable and upsetting thoughts. Whatever the experience, it's a fact that, by grace, a man (your father) was born with the ability to produce millions of life-giving seeds, and a blessed woman (your mother) was gifted an abundant yet set supply of reproductive eggs. They were physically brought together, and a miracle was made. Of the millions of sperm cells that race for the slight chance to be combined with one sacred egg, many come close, but only one gets to fertilize it. Out of those great numbers, *you* were the chosen one. That was a win.

The circumstances that brought your mother to the point of pregnancy may or may not have had anything to do with the showing of affection, love, or care, but the purpose behind your arrival was far greater than the conditions by which you came. You may have been adopted and not know all the details. You could have been taken in from a young age and raised by someone who was not familiar to you. Every situation is different. Thousands of babies are purposely left at hospitals each year or are found in settings not ideal for human life, abandoned by parents who are unwilling or unable to care for them. Then superheroes from across the globe in the form of garbage collectors, homeless people, community workers, and others on their daily routes are somehow led to the cries and moans heard from dark unseen corners. These innocent little lives are found and brought into emergency centers around the world, and thankfully many are nourished to full recovery. But what is it that kept them alive while they were left all alone, hungry, hurt, and afraid? How is it that some can survive extreme temperatures for days, often without clothing, and unable to crawl, walk, or speak for themselves? Who is it that protects them from being suffocated by trash or consumed by bulldozers? Maybe you were one of those abandoned babies, or perhaps you were raised in an environment where you felt completely neglected.

The beauty beyond all mysteries is that if you are reading (or listening to) these pages, you have survived to this point whatever life has thrown at you, and you are living proof of an invincible and loving provider who intended for you to be here.

Regardless of your introduction to planet Earth, you were hand-selected by the orchestrator of all time and space to make your grand appearance here. No person or authority has the right to treat you otherwise. You were born worthy, and everyone else in this world is too. If you are in any situation, relationship, or occupation where you are treated with anything less than fairness, kindness, humanity, and respect, it is not deserving of you. If it does not bring you peace or does not align with a positive outcome for you, it is likely not God's best for you. There are many times in my life when I've had to recalibrate and clear out things or people who were not serving my highest good. If the encounters were not positive and purpose-driven or did not reflect my morals and values, they were mere distractions from what I came to do. This sometimes applies to people you really like or care about. However, we did not exit our mother's womb in shackles. We were literally born free and worthy to be our best, which is our divine birthright. We must be deliberate about living and aligning ourselves in this way.

CHAPTER 2

DEMOGRAPHICS DO NOT DEFINE YOU

"At any given moment, you have the power to say: this is not how the story is going to end."

—CHRISTINE MASON MILLER

Had I accepted the statistics of the community I grew up in, I could have easily identified myself as one who was less likely to succeed. As a young black girl growing up in the South, I was raised by a single mother in a low-income community, and my father was nowhere in sight. He and my mother were never married. He fled the scene not long after I was born and started down a toxic path of getting arrested for multiple charges, leading him to spending many years in and out of prison.

My mother worked hard from the moment she graduated from high school, which was soon after giving birth to me. She started her very first job at Kentucky Fried Chicken. She did not have the luxury of taking a break. She got right to work, pulling shifts late into the night until closing before returning to my grandmother's house. My great-grandma also lived in the same neighborhood and helped split the task of looking after me most evenings while my mom was at work.

My mom eventually found a small house to rent about a block away. It was a tiny, tan-colored wooden house with a front screen door, double-bolt locks, and burglar bars on the windows. She did her best to make it a safe home. She placed chairs and heavy objects behind the door as an "alarm" to hear if someone tried to break in. I remember coming home each night. She searched the entire house before turning out all the lights once we were settled. We slept in the same bed, and she was always worried about keeping us safe. Our community had its share of drugs, crime, and gang violence. I recall there being an unidentified psychopath in the neighborhood who targeted women with obscene phone calls. Once my mother and I arrived home and turned out the lights, it was like clockwork. The phone started ringing. My mother tiptoed around the house, peeking behind the curtains because it was obvious we were being watched. One night she spotted a low-lit lamp through our neighbor's window that reflected the shadow of a man on a phone. My mother was terrified to learn that it was our neighbor! How creepy it was to know that someone next door was making these disturbing calls and could potentially harm us!

Soon we were able to move again. My grandmother got married and relocated with her new husband. My mother kept working, added a second job, and paid my grandmother rent for us to live in her former house. It was a small single-family home with a backyard and a giant old tree that stood directly over it. My grandmother started a new life. She no longer had to work and had a dedicated husband who took very good care of her. Together, they had a son my age named Cedric, who was like a brother to me. But he was my uncle, my mother's baby brother. Most evenings after school I stayed over at my grandma's until my mother got off work, and Cedric became my closest playmate. My grandma's house became my second home, and her husband became the only active grandfather in my life. He had his own business as a plumber. He was a contractor for the local community college and worked many other side jobs within the neighborhood. He was a jack-of-all-trades. He built Cedric and me seesaws and waterslides from scratch and even surprised us with pet rabbits during Easter time. He was a kind man and a hard worker.

My grandmother always cooked a hot fresh meal for dinner with a pan of sweet, buttery cornbread that tasted like pound cake. We all sat at her round kitchen table and ate together. She made sure I was fed, bathed, and ready for bed once my mother arrived from work. My mother would wake me after work, literally pick me up, and carry me over her shoulder to her little used Grand Prix. That part was healthy for me.

Times easily became stressful though, especially if something went wrong with the house and if my mom had to be late on the rent. I can recall one of the most hurtful things I ever heard in the late hours of the night. My grandma, in a very demeaning tone, hounded her about the rent or any other money she felt was due. Every time my mom made two steps forward, it seemed she had to take ten steps back. If it wasn't a problem with the maintenance of the house, it was something wrong with the car, the need for gas money, or something I needed for school. My grandmother seemed to have little or no compassion toward my mother. I could not understand how she could so easily talk down to my mom, her only daughter, who was working so hard and doing her best to raise me all by herself. Too often I witnessed one of the women who I loved so much, my grandma, verbally and emotionally tear down the one I loved the most, my mom. I could literally see my mother's unrest in always being made to feel that she "owed" my grandmother. I recall there were times when even my grandfather would politely ask my grandma to not be so hard on my mom. And although love was shown, unfortunately over the years I witnessed the on-and-off abrasive cycle continue. I later learned that this was a generational problem with some of the women in my family. They were particularly nonnurturing and ridiculed their daughters, yet they were more forgiving and showed more grace toward their sons. I knew early on that this was not something I wanted to represent, so I decided that I would always do my best to empathize with others and cheer them on—men included, but especially girls and women.

One night as my mother and I were sleeping, a loud roaring sound erupted as the ceiling of the room in which we slept nearly cracked wide open as the gigantic tree that stood directly over our house came crashing down into it! My heart nearly jumped out of my chest as I awoke thinking the world was coming to an end. My mother, who was in bed beside me, stood up and screamed, "Oh Lord, please protect us!" And sure enough, God did. Our sleeping room in the back of the house was dented, but it somehow held together and didn't collapse on top of us, while the front of the entire house was mostly ripped apart. The neighbors heard the huge collapse, and many stepped outside their homes to try to find out what was going on. Tears ran down my mother's face as she tried to comfort me. "It's the tree, but we are safe, and we're going to be OK." It was a huge setback for us, as the coming days and months would be filled with city workers and cleanup crews. My courageous mother made her way through the rubble to the front of the house to try to retrieve as many of our clothes, shoes, and my toys as possible before it was all plastered up. Thankfully, our little home was insured, as it took months for it to be repaired. Yet with limited options for temporary housing, my mother and I continued living in the house and found a way to be content in the remaining areas that were still functional while the rest was being repaired.

I was ashamed by the damage and the fact that we had to keep living in the house. It wasn't the easiest when a couple of my closest friends wanted to stop by, and I'd always find an excuse to not invite them. They lived in better-looking, more modern homes. Their parents drove nicer cars, and they were able to afford the latest style of clothes and designer brands. They always had big family gatherings, holiday parties, and a large selection of delicious food. They also had something extra-special that I did not—their dads. It always felt good visiting their homes. They seemed to have more fun and could relax knowing that there was an extra layer of security with their fathers there to support and provide for them. The feeling was always bittersweet. I felt so welcomed, but I knew that it was just a brief fantasy before I'd soon be returning home to my humble reality.

Despite the financial challenges, my mother instilled confidence in me. She managed to pull off what seemed to be miracles. She kept me clean and neatly dressed in bargain brands, mixing and matching pieces from different thrift shops. I psyched myself up to dislike the fashion trends that many of the other kids were wearing, and I did not ask for things I knew we could not afford. I became very comfortable wearing my own unique style. I received compliments at school on my outfits, and from that I learned that doing your own thing had value.

The ability to stay in your own lane and do your best with what you have in the moment is an asset. It builds character, strength, and patience. My mother worked, got off late, and picked me up from my grandma's every night. We arrived home, went to sleep fast, and rose early. She cooked breakfast, made sure I was neatly dressed, combed my hair, and got me off to school. She headed back to work, and we repeated the cycle. On my birthday, my mother managed to pull off the most decorative parties for me, and even though times were tough, I had some amazing Christmases with a beautifully decorated tree and many of my dream toys underneath. My mom also found other ways to make additional money; she sold candy and ice cream treats directly out of our side kitchen window to the kids in the neighborhood.

While there were many stressors growing up, I did not allow those demographics to define me. Something within me knew that even though my father never played his part and my mother had to make lemonade out of lemons, the journey had to get better. I learned to mentally thrive. I still excelled in school, and I held tight to the thing inside of me that never wavered—hope.

Regardless of your age, where you grew up, what you have or what condition you currently live in today, I encourage you to keep going because your surroundings are not the finish line. The statistics do not define your destiny. You must believe that no matter what the circumstances or the images around you, a better life is possible. You were born to win. Winners do the work and do not give up. My mother was the first example of what winning through perseverance looked like in my life.

CHAPTER 3

YOUR CHILDHOOD INTERESTS ARE LINKED TO YOUR PURPOSE

"Every child you encounter is a divine appointment."

—WESS STAFFORD

We all have gifts and talents that are unique and tailor made to our personalities. It is sometimes difficult to identify what your purpose is and how to go about finding it. We did not enter this life with an instruction manual, but the infinite one gave us all that we could ever need. Did you know that the one who created us speaks the languages of all life? Including those of babies and children? How magnificent is that?

I spent a lot of time alone growing up. I did not have any siblings and was the only little girl in my family. I had an all-boy cousin crew who were good playmates during my visits to my great-grandma's house, and there was Cedric, my mother's baby brother, whom I was closest to. We went to the same schools and played a lot together. We rode our bikes along the back dirt roads, popped wheelies, went skating, flew kites, played baseball, and went fishing in ditch holes for crawfish. Although I enjoyed learning and hanging out with the boys in my family, it was still sometimes difficult for me to find satisfying play, so I would escape to being solo. My grandmother's backyard and the woods behind her house were my adventurous playing field. I climbed the fruit trees and picked figs, peaches, and pears, literally eating them with grime still on the peel. I picked pecans and ate them for snacks. At times, I would imagine I was a superhero girl. Running through the crackling leaves in the fall, I tried to catch the squirrels and rabbits. I truly enjoyed this. It was just me in God's rustic nature. Because I was an only child, this was my main playtime outside, except during recess breaks at school with other kids.

Life at home with my mom was pretty sheltered. I did not watch a lot of television or movies growing up. I never really had friends over, sleepovers, or any kind of *over* for that matter, except for those I would create over and over in my imagination. I believed this to be all a part of my mother's unwavering aim at keeping me safe. However, the beauty of this rigid and protective life was that I learned to improvise. I learned early on how to be comfortable just being alone, finding my own self-play and discovery. I gathered my dolls, crayons, pens, chalk, and whatever I could find to write on. I scribbled letters, words, sentences, and constructed entire lectures (in my head, that is), for the imaginary audience I had created. I remember often I would shut myself off in an empty room and simply go all in with my "talk." Where I learned this from, I cannot recall, but the gibberish I was saying was very real to me. When I was caught by my mom or grandma, they humorously said I was "playing teacher." I could do this for hours because it was fulfilling and felt very natural for me. Also, my "audience" happened to be very good company.

Before getting tainted by societal views, children are the latest and greatest arrivals fresh out of spirit form. Therefore, the purity of your childhood represents the time frame when it is easiest for you to convert your innate knowledge from God into that which is conceivable to humanity. You were likely not able to articulate this knowing, but something within you was drawn to things that represented who and what you were supposed to do here—and chances are, you were fearless about it. Consider this. A child is drawn to Lego blocks and spends hours attempting to build something magical in their eyes. When the supply runs out, they beg you to purchase more blocks so they can keep building. They are not interested in any other toys other than those that allow their ability to configure objects perfectly into a certain form. Pay attention—might this be an architect in the making? The same goes for a child who is drawn to dolls, and you notice that their ability to style and restyle the doll's clothing brings them the greatest joy. They continue asking you to buy more doll clothes to keep their creativity going. Might this child be a future fashion designer? These are just simple examples so that you might pay closer attention to the divine signals that are always trying to express through us from the time we are born.

For me, it was always trying to find something on which I could write. Even as I grew and learned to type, I was excited to find another method of getting words onto a page using different fonts and symbols. I found the ability to communicate came naturally for me. School assignments that involved writing papers were often an area others struggled in, but for me this was a strength. I now know that these gifts were linked to my future self who in various ways would share inspiration through the spoken and written word.

Whatever our purpose (not necessarily just one thing), it is given to us to be shared for the greater good. Your reward comes because of you being your authentic self, honoring your gifts, and following that inner call. And please know that while formal education can be a positive tool to assist you on your journey, having a certificate or degree does not automatically equate to living a life filled with purpose. If you can focus on doing the thing that truly lights you up from the inside, a win will be yours.

I know that life happens, and it may take some time to get back to that state of remembering things from early on. Our calling could be one or many things during different seasons of our lives. One of the most important things we can do for ourselves is to take the time to discover what it is that we were created to do. For years, I felt that my chosen career as a nurse had nothing to do with my calling. I realize this is a problem for so many. Regardless of where you are in your life, the fact remains that if you are breathing, there is a special reason that you are still here at this present moment. How loving is it to know that the Creator, who is in spirit form, selected you to carry out a dream in human form to make this world a better place?

If you don't know where to begin finding clarity, I invite you to get really still and think back to your childhood. What were you passionate about? What things or objects were you drawn to? Who motivated or inspired you? What were they doing that you loved so much? What was it that you would have done had you been able to freely choose? What were you interested in that may have been considered weird to your family or friends? What did you wish to do that was unpopular? Who did you want to be but were afraid of being judged? These are just some examples of where you might want to start. Whatever you do well is also a divine clue!

I know there are many religious, cultural, and societal pressures that can cause you to nearly sabotage yourself and conform to who or what everyone else thinks you should be. However, winning is about saying yes to your truest, highest self and using this one human experience that you have been given to live fully! I have a friend who grew up extremely poor. His passion from childhood was to become rich, and through faith, perseverance, and hard work that is exactly what he did. Today, he consults others on how to find their path to financial freedom. It is important to always remember that our childhood interests are divine signposts as to what we came here to do. If you get lost along the way, it is something you can always refer to and help find your way back to your truth.

CHAPTER 4

YOUR EXPERTISE BEGINS IN YOUR ENVIRONMENT

"Environment is the invisible hand
that shapes human behavior."

—JAMES CLEAR

Never underestimate the power to be gained from the environment you were born into or currently find yourself in. Your worth is not defined by your environment, but your purpose in this life is enhanced by it. What I mean by this is simple. Your environment is your experience. That which you are most familiar with becomes an area of expertise. This has nothing to do with formal education or training. You do not have to have a degree to be an expert. If you pay close attention, you will find that many of your life experiences, both positive and negative, were aligned so that you could use them one day to help someone.

I did not recall seeing my father again until he came to visit when I was hospitalized in the second grade. He did not stay long before taking off again, and I was very nervous and distrustful of him. His energy was sly, and something within me was resistant to allowing him to even get close to me.

I was in the hospital for minor surgery, though for me, it seemed quite major. All I knew at that time was that the diagnosis was something common in children my age. It caused a dysfunction in the urinary system and left me feeling as though my bladder was always full. It was very nerve-racking for a seven-year-old to endure. I had become anxious at school and would literally run out of class after being told that I could not go to the restroom until next break. My teachers did not understand it and would dismiss me when I'd ask to go several times in a row. After being told no, I'd start crying and run off to the restroom anyway. I was a well-behaved student, so my teachers knew this was unusual for me. It was a horrible experience physically and psychologically because every time I would run to the restroom, my classmates would start laughing at me. Within a couple of weeks, it escalated to me being sent to the principal's office.

My grandmother had a talk with the principal and picked me up from school that day. My mom took me to the doctor and discovered the issue. Today, I know that I had a UPJ (uteropelvic junction) obstruction, which means the tubes leading from my kidneys to my bladder were blocked. The procedure I had to correct this was a pyeloplasty. My mother was told by the doctor that if I did not have the surgery, I would be at high risk of needing dialysis for the rest of my life. Thank God she agreed to it, and my surgery was successful. I recovered well with no further issues after that. My teachers and principal were very supportive, and I remember them bringing get-well gifts to the hospital and a packet with all my assignments so I wouldn't get behind in my schoolwork.

Interestingly, it was during that hospitalization and the visits from a very sweet caregiver named Patty, that I first learned about her role—*a nurse!* At the time, there was no thought in my mind that I'd ever become one, but it was a positive experience that I clearly remembered—feeling safe, cared for, and in good hands. I have been a patient a few times in my life, and it always stood out when I was treated with gentleness and kindness. Once I became a nurse, I remembered this and wanted to be certain that the patients I took care of knew that they were genuinely understood and supported. By the time I was ready to move on to middle school, my mother and several other parents within our community learned of a new middle school that was opening in one of the suburbs of the city. It had a school bus stop on the corner of my street. The school was believed to offer a better education and was considered a good option for students from my neighborhood who met all the criteria. My mother applied for my enrollment, and I was accepted as a first-time student to Donnie Bickham Middle School. A year earlier, Cedric had been fortunate enough to get accepted to a highly esteemed magnet school across town. We both took entrance exams, but I did not score high enough. Therefore, I was excited to try the new school. My only other option would have been to attend the only middle school that was in my district, which had a reputation for high crime due to the hostile juvenile behavior and gang activity in the area. It was not only risky for students, but for the teachers as well.

Overall, I adjusted to the new school. It allowed me a little more exposure to diversity, which gave me somewhat a mini glance of the real world. It was not exactly perfect. I remember getting bullied along the way and dodging people who were seemingly harsh for no reason. It was at that stage, in the sixth grade, that I first learned about racism, and I found myself having to escape a few racial riots that took place after school. It started with rumors that "a riot was happening at 3 p.m.," which was organized by a group of all-white eighth grade boys who boldly identified themselves as "children of the KKK." It was at that time that I quickly learned about the history of the Ku Klux Klan! As the final bell rang, I ran as fast as I could to my school bus, dodging the rocks that were being thrown at black students. They made it clear that we were not welcome. They yelled, "Get out of our neighborhood, get out of our school!"

While running I was pushed down on the sidewalk, and I was badly bruised. It was very frightening, and the school's leadership made it clear that this type of behavior would not be tolerated. The students who organized the riots were placed on suspension and security was heightened with local police officers, who became a part of the school's staff. Thankfully, I was able to keep moving forward and apply myself to the classwork and various styles of teaching. I walked away a B student.

Once ninth grade arrived, I returned to school in my neighborhood to complete three and a half years at Green Oaks High. It was the same high school my mother had graduated from, and the place where, years before, she met my father.

Ironically, by the time I started my freshman year, my mother had made her way back to the high school as well. But this time, she had gotten a job working part-time in the school's cafeteria. She worked at the school part-time during the day and at a local casino at night.

Cedric and I would become classmates again. He had graduated from middle school a year earlier and was a sophomore. We both found ourselves at the same high school participating in activities together. He played the drums, and I later became a majorette in the high school marching band.

As I grew older, my needs became greater. I became an A student and was more involved in extracurricular activities. This required a greater need for money. I was a member of several organizations at school and within the community. I became a cheerleader. I also participated in several pageants and won a few. This made my mother smile. I loved and respected my mother so much, and I never wanted to humiliate her by asking for more than we could afford. I tried to downplay my interests in the activities and was always willing to opt out to save money, but my mother insisted I take part.

The stress of all of it weighed heavy on her. And while she encouraged and supported my participation, my mother started to become bitter. She had pressed so hard to get us both to a point of stability but had also sacrificed her own youth for the hope and sake of mine.

She slowly began to uncover a very private, yet unresolved pain that she had held in for so long. And in every moment of her release, I felt it. Verbally, psychologically, and emotionally, I witnessed my mother go through the long-term side effects of what had been a heavy dose of her hardship. I felt that she resented me. As a result, my relationship with my mother became a rocky rollercoaster. I had just reached the same age she had become pregnant with me. However, my life was looking very different. I had such a happy and outgoing personality, and the more I came out of my shell and into an awareness of life and how I dreamed of pursuing it, the worse things got. I naturally started shifting from her views on life and was developing my own. It started to feel like thinking for myself was a sin. How dare I dream? How dare I imagine a better life for myself? How dare I even laugh too hard and express a sense of joy? With each new accomplishment, it seemed I could no longer be authentically celebrated. For every positive, she had a negative. When I developed friends, a boyfriend, mentors, or any positive relationship, she seemed to envy the fact that I might end up somehow enjoying life more than she did. When there was just a tiny spark of inspiration in my eyes, she quickly dampened it with a negative comment. Perhaps it was because her little girl was growing up, and she felt that she could no longer protect me. Or perhaps it was because she had conquered motherhood so young and had put in all the work on her own, and she was devastated by the thought that she might somehow be separated from the one thing she had to show for it—me.

My mother had worked so hard from the moment I was born and had not stopped to smell the roses. This made me very sad, and it became my silent pain. I felt indebted to her. There were times when she gave me public praise around family or friends, but in private I was verbally attacked and criticized. Whenever I tried to initiate a conversation about my feelings and try to get her to understand how she was hurting me, I was often shunned, and my mother was in constant denial about her behavior toward me.

I developed anxiety and started to become very nervous about doing even the basic things, like making my bed perfectly or folding the towels just right. I sometimes felt like the character Christina Crawford in the movie, *Mommie Dearest*. I loved my mom so much and wanted so badly for her to be happy and proud of me. I knew she loved me, too, but over time it seemed that nothing I did was good enough. I soon recognized that this was a part of a generational "curse" that I knew I had to break. The dysfunctional and emotionally abusive patterns that I had observed from early on in my grandmother's behavior toward my mother had recycled, and I started to experience the same behavior from my mother toward me. Again and again, I made a pact with myself. *This will* not *be me.* Through my observations, experiences, prayers, and insight, I became determined to break that cycle. I knew that I was innocent and had not done anything to deserve to be treated that way. At that point in my life, I established a principle that I still live by today. I made the commitment that I would never behave that way toward any child or other living being! I am grateful to have broken that curse and to still uphold that.

Your environment is not only a physical place, but also a mental state. One who lives the environment is gifted with the expertise of it, although at the time it may not feel like a gift at all! I can easily speak about the challenges of growing up as a fatherless daughter by having been one. I never knew what it was like to have my father be there for me, so I had no other choice but to learn to succeed in life without him. I do not hold a badge of honor because of this, but I am a product of growing up in this way. So I can encourage those who may feel that they cannot thrive because of this same circumstance to keep going. Unfortunately, I have also learned from ongoing experiences, personally and professionally, how to navigate life as a black person in a society embedded by racism. From a young age, as far back as middle school to this present day, I encounter it. It has been a lifelong journey. For me, no matter the form, racism is easily recognizable. It is felt before spoken; it is seen piercing through the eyes. It is exuded like missiles from the heart. It is taught, learned, and often passed down and carried out by the offspring. To be racist is also a choice. You get to choose if you want to harshly contribute to society in this way, or to consciously stop the centuries-old vicious cycle that may have been handed down to you. This also applies to family constructs, in which toxic patterns have repeated themselves. We can all choose to be more loving and overcome the negative behaviors that may have been demonstrated by those who have come before us. Whatever environment you find yourself in does not necessarily mean that you chose it or expected it. But know that you are accountable for how well you respond and navigate its course. This is where you become the expert.

CHAPTER 5

YOUR SKIN COLOR IS DIVINE

"Color is a fact. Race is a social construct."

—ISABEL WILKERSON

"Nigger nurse! You nigger nurse! I don't want this nigger taking care of me!" a patient yelled at the top of her voice as I walked in to introduce myself. She quickly pressed the call light and started screaming, "Get this nigger out of here!" I remember how ugly this behavior felt, and it was not uncommon in one of the small predominantly white east Texas towns where I was completing one of my clinical rotations. It did not help that the charge nurse, house supervisor, and my preceptor (the nurse I was shadowing for the day) all had the same skin color as the patient—white. My plea that someone would listen to my side of the story in that moment was quickly brushed off. I tried to explain how I had just met the patient, and from the moment she saw me, she became enraged. After that, I immediately turned around and exited the room. Her yelling had caused a scene and it was as if I had done something to harm her as I walked out and was met with flat stares by staff and visitors who were on the unit.

The charge nurse who had made the assignment seemed to have no regard for my position or feelings as I tried to explain what happened. Her first reaction was to yell, "What did you do to her?" I started to say *nothing*, but she abruptly interrupted by saying, "OK, just move on! She's just having a bad day!" She then quickly reassigned me to another patient and assigned one of my classmates, who happened to be white, to care for that patient instead. In that moment, I would have really appreciated if someone would have taken the time to simply check in on how I was feeling. Instead, I was expected to just forget about the incident and move on. The nursing leaders were not easily approachable, and I did not have an ally. I felt negatively seen, unsupported and silenced. Yet, I had to suppress my upset and try to keep going to finish my clinical day. My whole body constricted and felt robotic as I tried to move on to the next patient, while counting down the hours until I could run out of that hospital and clinical rotation for good! This is just one of the numerous times in my life that I've experienced prejudice and discrimination from my white counterparts in the health-care environment. This can have such an ugly impact in an atmosphere where healing should be the focus. I inserted this incident here to acknowledge another key component in understanding the depth of your worth.

Designed by God and often cursed by society, depending on its color, we wear a miraculous covering which happens to be the largest organ of the human body: skin. If you have a problem with your own or any other person's skin color, then you have a problem with the source of all creation. The Creator designed it just for you. We must wear it and care for it with pride because we are all unique expressions of the most high.

Whatever you are purposed to do on this earth, is meant to happen in the skin that God gave you. Society might try to make you believe otherwise, but it is not so. For those of you who, like me, were gifted with one of the many beautiful, rich brown skin tones—ranging from deep dark to bright reddish and yellow-brown—embrace the fact that you were wonderfully made in God's rainbow of life, no matter how society tries to exclude you from it.

Due to the colorism present in this world, it is important that you know and always remember that whatever your skin color, it is a part of your unique divine design. It goes hand in hand with the confidence in knowing that the Creator intended for you to be incarnated this way. You were born worthy in the skin that you came in (and so was every other human being on the planet).

This world continues to bear the heavy burden of the centuries-old evils of racial discrimination, inequality, prejudice, bigotry, and bias, which cause the many man-made poisonous stereotypes, injustices, and systemic thought patterns that brutally and corruptly run through our society. Such hate and evil have caused multitudes of diseases and enormous death. Not until the mindset of the wicked converts to love and understands the worthiness of all, will the deadly cycle end. This change can only happen from *within*.

If you struggle with being racist or prejudiced, I challenge you to consider how you can be more loving. You must first be honest with yourself. Ask yourself: How do I truly feel when I see a black, brown, or other person who does not have the same skin color or physical characteristics as me? At the bank? In the workplace? Walking or jogging in my neighborhood? Do my thoughts automatically shift to fear or negativity? Do I feel that they are of lesser value? If so, where did I acquire my belief system about this group? Who taught me this? Would I want someone to feel or treat me this way based on how I look and how God made me? How can I shift my thoughts and actions in a more positive direction to change this?

You can serve as game changers and allies right where you are. Black and brown people have been historically the most persecuted in all humanity—blatantly murdered and mistreated. When you can, show up, speak up, and lift those who have been sufferers of a man-made construct and experienced the most harsh and inhumane treatment in the land. Skin color is an instant identifier that provides many a privilege, and I encourage you to use that privilege to positively serve. You can start right in your homes by how you teach your children, dismantling the negative conditioning that may have been generationally taught and passed down to you. As individuals, you are highly capable and have the ability inside of you to make a profound and lasting impact. But herein lies the most vital question to ask yourself: Do I choose to?

Whatever skin encompasses you, God blessed you with it to navigate in this world in your uniqueness. No matter what your outer covering is, your soul is pleased to be represented by you! It is your choice to align with your soul's mission, which is always linked to love.

CHAPTER 6

YOUR BODY IS A LUXURIOUS VEHICLE

"The greatest miracle on earth is the human body. It is stronger and wiser than you may realize, and improving its ability to self heal is within your control."

—DR. FABRIZIO MANCINI

When I wake up each day, I open my mouth and say, "thank you." I know that I have been given another sweet opportunity to live, move, and be a part of this once-in-a-lifetime human experience. Divine intelligence made it so that trillions of cells could be brought together in perfect order to form the organs, tissues, and systems which make up the miraculous human body—a priceless gift! The body is not the totality of who we are, but it is the container that God provided us to transport ourselves for the course of this lifetime. It is original and made of the highest quality elements, and it requires premium fuel for its lasting beauty and sustainability. This anatomical force is the finest, most luxurious vehicle on the planet, and it is our responsibility to maintain it!

There is nothing man-made that could ever equate to the God-given machine that the human body is. As newborns and children, it is the responsibility of our parents or caregivers to ensure that we are properly nourished, but as we grow into adults, the responsibility becomes our own. Whatever you place in your body impacts your entire life!

I grew up in a community where access to affordable, nutritious food was limited. Quality supermarkets and health food stores with fresh organic foods were not in my neighborhood. The few that existed required driving across town and paying a higher cost, which we could not afford. Instead, there were plenty of quick-fix, fast foods, chicken joints, burger shacks, and a multitude of gas stations and liquor stores. We were traditional, lived in the South and were just grateful to have food and good flavor. Therefore, I grew up on the Standard American Diet (SAD), consisting of foods high in sugar, salt, animal products, red meat, processed meats, high-fat dairy, refined carbohydrates, sodas, and fast foods. On average, my breakfast consisted of grits, eggs, and toast with sausage, bacon, or ham. My lunch was mostly provided by whatever was on the menu at the school cafeteria, and dinner at my grandma's always included a meat such as chicken, pork chops, or spaghetti with meatballs and cornbread. I did not have any examples of what adequate nutrition or regular exercise looked like. It was not until I became a young adult that I began thinking about exercise and making healthier food choices. I realized that my youth was on my side, but only for a short while. If I wanted to be healthy for the long run, I knew I would eventually need to make some serious changes to what I was eating and develop and maintain a more physically active lifestyle.

I have learned that there is a direct connection between the foods we consume and how we feel and function in our daily lives. If you think about the journey it took for your food to get onto your plate, you might reconsider what you want and need to take in. This goes beyond the physical journey of your food and includes the emotional and spiritual transfer.

From the fish of the sea to the flock in the air, and all the animals of this God-given land, their lives matter too. Animals are life forms with bodies, personalities, and feelings. Their presence is vital and supports the continuation of our ecosystem. However, they are often taken for granted, neglected, mistreated, and slaughtered for many forms of human use and ultimately for consumption—on your plate! That is, unless you choose differently. Can you imagine the relationship between a live being that was potentially sick, crying, and in pain before its death, and the stressful energy of that being transferred to you upon eating it? How might that impact human behaviors and health long term if this is an ongoing daily practice? In addition to the many diseases that are caused by stress, negative thought patterns, sedentary lifestyles etc., I believe it is a valid conclusion that you do become, in essence, what you eat. There is no judgment here of whatever your personal choice. I am simply giving you a gentle nudge to think deeper about the effects of what you put in your body and how well it functions, and to consider how you can lead a healthier, more whole life starting with what you eat and how you treat your miraculous body.

Today, I live a plant-based lifestyle. It took milestones to get here. I went through lots of trial and error on my quest to have more energy and live more ethically. I had many cycles of back and forth trying various detoxes, fasts, and cleansing programs only to clear my system temporarily and get right back on the toxic rollercoaster ride of pure junk! It was not until I became sick of my own self and how tired I was feeling that I finally sought the expertise of a holistic health practitioner. She offered great insight and a meaningful plan, which consisted of not only the health of my body, but also that of my mind and spirit. I was finally able to understand and put into practice the tools to improve the interconnectedness of my whole being. We took small steps to gradually remove the harmful elements of my diet and incorporated more dense nutrients and supplements to support me on the path. This also included identifying and slowly removing myself from people and environments that did not support my healthier, higher self. Within days, then weeks and months, the journey got easier. I became more accountable, trusted myself more, and learned greater discipline. It has been one of the best choices that I have made for myself, and I continue to grow and expand in my profession from that foundation. Over time I became more calm, vibrant, alert, and happy, and I know for sure that my body is much stronger and healthier because of the plentiful life-giving fuel that I feed it and how intentional I am about moving and caring for it.

In a kinder and more merciful world, we could all be enjoying the benefits of life-giving foods, our diets high in organic fruits, vegetables, whole grains, legumes, beans, nuts, and seeds. We could save innocent beings from harsh treatment and slaughter. We would experience the plethora of high-frequency plant food options, loaded with nature's finest ingredients, vital nutrients, wonderful textures, and delicious flavors. We would walk, run, dance, and exercise more! We would enjoy the positive electric charge of filling ourselves up by drinking bountiful alkaline water to keep our cells happy and hydrated. We would let our food be our medicine and prevent and reverse many bodily ailments, cancers, and disease! Eating life promotes more life; eating death promotes more death. In a practical and gentler world, if we choose, we *can* tap into the joy of greater health, wholeness, sustained energy, vitality, and longevity, which are beautiful results of eating, drinking, and living in a way that is ethical, affordable, compassionate, and humane, with no compromise of *life*! If you love and care for your luxurious body, it will graciously love you back.

PART TWO

YOUR WILL (INTENTION)

WINNING STARTS WITH YOUR INTENTION

.

CHAPTER 7

LET YOUR INTENTIONS BE OF GOODWILL

"Goodwill is the one and only asset that competition cannot undersell or destroy."

—MARSHALL FIELD

To be alive on planet Earth means you are given a second-by-second, minute-by-minute, day-by-day opportunity to be grateful for yourself and others, near and far, who make up the global citizenship. If you are viewing any other person, nationality, color, race, or sex as faulty, unworthy, less than or beneath your own, then this equates to betrayal of the person in the mirror. Why betrayal? If you were loved, gifted, and trusted to come to the planet, yet you arrive and spew out judgment or hate, then how can you be used for the greater good? Before you set out to do anything, if you are in a state of rage, envy, vengeance, meanness, gossip, evil, or jealousy etc., your intentions are all bad. Your intention determines your future.

Before you commit any act, ask yourself these questions: Am I seeking to offer help, peace, joy, kindness, or love? Is the outcome of my actions going to cause pain or suffering to someone? If so, is there a better choice that I can make? Are my actions good and fair? Intention is spiritual law. Whatever you set out to be your end goal in any situation, you will reap from that core desire in your heart. That is your intention. It does not matter if you say that you did not intend to do a thing. Spirit always knows the truth of what is in your heart. Your intention is the thought that occurs before you take any action. Therefore, if you seek to cause harm or suffering of any kind to another being, without reasonable cause (i.e., to defend yourself) then your intentions are not of goodwill.

People often ask me how I always seem so joyful. How is it that when others lack patience and tolerance, I can remain so calm? How is it that I am always so positive? I attribute this to a few things. In each of the earthly titles I hold—a woman, a black person, a health-care professional, a daughter, a friend etc.—I have at some point been marginalized or mistreated. Things also did not come easy for me; I learned how to wait for things I longed for the most. My journey has taught me how to be patient and kind and loving and grateful, and I can wholeheartedly say that my intentions are always good. That is my core! I have no desire to cause harm to myself or any person or life force that exists. There is a grace that comes with that. This starts with what some might consider small things. Think about your daily interactions. Do you have road rage? Are you a person who acts like a bully when you are driving? Do you take pride in honking your horn nonstop when the person ahead of you does not move within seconds of the traffic light turning from red to green? If so, what is the reason behind that? Do you lack patience? Are you angry? Where are you going that requires such rocket speed? What if the person in front of you were lost and trying to find their way? What if they are not feeling well? Of course, there is no way for you to know this, but it is something to remember and consider the next time you have a moment of rage—on and off the road.

Despite all the corruption and discord that could happen in any environment, because I keep my intentions in the right state, there is a peace that abides within me, a protection that covers me, and divine favor that meets me. This does not mean that bad things do not happen to good people, but when good people show up with good intentions, good things happen. If you can intend well, you will live in peace. You can walk the corridors of life knowing that you have sown good seeds, your heart is whole, and your soul is satisfied. I know for many that is easier said than done, which brings me to my next topic: the author of goodwill, God.

CHAPTER 8

GETTING TO KNOW THE CREATOR (GOD)

"Most of us know about God, but that is quite different from knowing God."

—BILLY GRAHAM

I could not have made it at any point in my life without someone before me and then myself (after becoming me) believing that there was something greater, higher, and more powerful than me that I could absolutely depend on.

Allow me to introduce the ultimate foundation of living from the mindset and will of good (God). If you are not a religious person or perhaps not exposed to the practice of a faith, I am not here to offer you religion. I am here to introduce you to the source of all peace, love, joy, healing, and recovery, so that you may find rest.

I know that of the deep corners of the earth offer different cultures, religions, and belief systems, including individuals who may have chosen not to participate in any of them. I understand all too well the many sides of this. As we grow, we learn, and if we choose, we continue to evolve. In most circumstances, we start out by adopting whatever religion or belief system we were born into. We naturally follow whatever our family believes, and along with that usually comes a specific set of morals and values, or rules. For example, if I would have been born on the continent of Asia, I would have likely grown up as Muslim, Hindu, Buddhist, or Sikh. However, I grew up in North America in the southern state of Louisiana in what is known as the Bible Belt, a region known for having the most Christian churches combined, exceeding the national average! As we grow, we typically choose our native faith to live by, or we expand our knowledge to include greater truths that fully aligns and agrees with our soul. I was born into the Christian faith; today, I still identify with that and live my life from the foundation of biblical text. Furthermore, my journey of faith expanded far beyond my childhood views, and as I grew, I gained further insights that truly resonated from a more spiritual—versus religious—understanding of God. I took God out of the box of a building and realized that God is everywhere—in, through, as, and around us. Wherever we are, God is.

In my youth, my mother and grandmother introduced me to the local church. It was a traditional Baptist church within our neighborhood. Cedric and I started out by attending Sunday school. We participated in small, early-morning classes divided by age groups. The classes were separate from the sanctuary and taught by elders of the church. Upon arrival, we were each handed the weekly lesson in a small booklet and were offered a snack—usually saltine crackers with water or juice. I remember the classrooms being cold and the crackers being stale. Though I didn't complain much, I recall thinking, *I wish someone would turn on the heat—if there is any heat. And I wonder if they know these crackers are stale?* Those same crackers would eventually be served during communion with grape juice, so I started to believe they had more of an "ancient" flavor to go along with the sacred history of my Sunday school lessons. I mostly enjoyed meeting and mingling with the kids in my class. Otherwise, I found myself bored and never really picked up my souvenir Sunday school books again. We also attended vacation bible school, which usually occurred for about a week in the summer. For me it was OK, but I mainly looked forward to getting a new T-shirt and seeing what snacks would be offered.

After a while, Cedric and I joined the youth choir. He eventually started playing the drums alongside the choir. We attended services faithfully every Sunday. The service was orderly, and everything happened according to schedule—the singing of the choir, the announcements, the sermon, the offering, and the benediction. I listened closely as the pastor preached messages from the Bible, and in my childhood mind, I took the meaning and interpretation of those messages *literally*. "Ask and it is given." I remember asking God to let Michael Jackson be at my house when I returned home after church. When this didn't happen, I thought I had not prayed hard enough. "Read your Bible daily." I recall receiving my very first Holy Bible as a gift from the church after I was baptized. The Bible was white with my name printed in gold letters. I started to read it daily and became anxious because I didn't know how much I was supposed to read before stopping each day. I would start crying in panic if I did not think I had covered enough chapters in order to make God happy. "Pray without ceasing." I started to feel guilty if I forgot to say the Lord's Prayer every day—and to say it several times a day! My mother tried to reassure me that God was very understanding if I didn't get around to praying and reading my Bible each day. The pastor's messages were intended to be motivating, but the delivery at times seemed more fear based. It was sometimes difficult as a child trying to comprehend without walking away afraid.

I was taught that I was born a sinner (ungodly person) and needed to be purged from my sins (the sin I was born into and the immoralities I might commit throughout my life). Heaven was deemed a magical and holy place far beyond the sky, where we all had a chance to go and live peacefully forever when we die. In contrast, there was hell and its CEO, the devil. Hell was described as a place of eternal fiery flames, deep beyond the dark pits of the earth, which was run by the evil one, the devil, who roamed the planet and had been given permission by God to punish those who did bad things. I believed that the Bible had somehow been left here by God and that it was meant for everyone to follow line by line. If we were too far off, we'd have a greater chance of slipping into hell when we die. I knew I did *not* want that! I also knew that I never wanted to even come close to meeting or spending any kind of time with the devil.

I had conflicting and mixed feelings about what I was learning, and at times I was scared out of my mind. But since my family seemed to be on the straight and narrow path, I figured so was I. In my limited view, getting to heaven was a huge and rightful challenge, and getting sent to hell was terribly a lot easier. I found myself worried about both.

What resonated and felt mostly right was my understanding of God the Almighty, whose power stretched far and wide beyond the planets and the entire solar system. He is spirit responsible for the creation of all things and people, including me. I believed God to be the maker of miracles, who placed the beautiful rainbows in the sky after a storm, and the one that I could call upon for help when I needed guidance or was in trouble. I was at total peace with this awareness, and from the time I was a child I somehow felt was true.

Later, I was formally introduced to Jesus, the Christ who was sent by God, born in the flesh like me and who had lived on earth like me. During His time on earth, He experienced the many trials that humanity would bring. And as a representative of all humankind, He faced much adversity, yet He embraced people from all walks of life unconditionally and unapologetically. He went about His business working, healing, and helping others, even those who were judged and viewed unworthy. He uplifted them and made them unashamed. He became their friend. He was honest and kind and was followed by multitudes. He brought the light that the world needed. Yet He still experienced being hated and rejected. He endured betrayal and brutality. He was whipped and beaten and mocked by his enemies. And ultimately, crucified. Leading right up to His death, He was made fun of by His adversaries, as they did not believe that He was king. They placed a crown of thorns on His head, and while beating Him, they led Him through the city of Jerusalem until He reached Golgotha, also known as Calvary. As they nailed Him by His wrists and feet to a wooden cross, He was lifted high on His death post for all the crowd to see, and with one final spear thrusted into his chest, blood and water flowed after He took His final breath. Upon dying in the flesh, He soon resurrected in spirit, fulfilling His mission to humanity—to redeem a hurting world.

Many historical accounts of this have been recorded. Some of them documented a similar narrative of the Messiah, yet the *being* Himself was translated as alternate names. The Bible is the most known record. Centuries and centuries would pass, yet the power of the message has withstood the test of time, never to be destroyed. There is something otherworldly about that. Jesus shared a final prophecy before His death. At His last meal, He served bread and wine to all who gathered. He stated: "This is my body (bread), broken for you" (1 Corinthians 11:24). And "this is my blood (wine), which is poured out for you" (Matthew 26:28). His body represented our flesh; His bloodshed and death represented our humanly hardship. He was the sacrificial lamb of life, and His resurrection represented our eternal home—with God, from whom we came and to whom we return. He is the great example of unconditional love. His teachings and actions represented that. I believed His mission as true, and during an altar call, I publicly stood before the church and professed.

The Prayer to Accept Jesus
Dear Jesus,
I confess all my faults, and I repent of them.
I ask for Your forgiveness.
I believe that your life, death, and resurrection represented me.
I invite You to come into my heart.
I accept You as my Lord and Savior.
Thank You.
Amen.

I believed this prayer and received it as my gift of salvation. I understood that it did not have to be made public, and even if said in private it still held true. For me, it represented giving my life back to God, therefore being *born again* (or beginning again). The following week, I was baptized in water, which symbolized being cleansed and starting anew. Therefore, Jesus was my path to God. His teachings promote living a life of purpose, goodwill, and love.

If you struggle in your thoughts or belief about who or what God is, I invite you to just ask. Ask the Creator for answers, and you will find them. I know that this may not be easy, considering you may not have had a conversation with pure spirit before, but I can assure you that there is absolutely nothing to be afraid of, and I believe you will find the experience to be quite positive. So, when you are ready, this will help you start the conversation. Get comfortable. Take a deep breath, then exhale, and another inhale and exhale, and just one more. Now, open your mouth, and with your heart, speak these words:

Dear Creator (God),
I am not sure what to believe about You, but I
am very interested in knowing the truth.
I ask that You guide me and reveal to me in
ways that only I would best understand.
I open my heart and mind to receive all the
answers that I could ever need.
Please help me to find the way, the truth, and
the life, so that I may go forth and fulfill
my purpose, from a heart that is *all* good.
And so it is. Amen.

Now believe that you have been heard, and watch the answers come.

CHAPTER 9

HURT ATTRACTS
HUMAN ANGELS

"Angels are the dispensers and administrators
of the divine beneficence toward us."

—JOHN CALVIN

When you are hurting, God will send earth angels to uplift and help you. My high school years went well academically, but otherwise were emotionally draining. It was very difficult for me to fit in with my peers. I was never a follower, so instead of going along with the crowd, I kept to myself and did my own thing. In addition to not having the emotional support I needed in my home environment, I had to deal with the toxicity of the mean girls at school. I became confident being alone and was content staying to myself. When I eventually developed a few good friends, they were a sweet bonus!

As I walked the hallway of my high school headed to class, the smile that I wore on the outside did not get past a set of wise eyes that could somehow see my discouragement on the inside. Mr. Wesley, a tall, distinguished teacher, stood in the hallway of his assigned wing. Every time we met, he had an uplifting word. "You are such a neat young lady." "You carry yourself with such poise." "You are bright, and you are qualified to go far, remember that." He became my most influential teacher. Leading a class far beyond the required course work, he taught lessons of hope, offered encouragement, and humorously demonstrated love. Mr. Wesley was just one of the many angels who would begin to present themselves with pertinent life lessons for the journey ahead.

It was in my junior year that I learned I qualified to graduate a semester early due to my high performance in advanced English class. I started to think about what I should do with the extra time. I decided I had two options. One was to find a job or take advantage and start some early college courses. I ended up doing both. I was in the top 5 percent of my graduating class, and while it was expected by my teachers and peers that I would for sure go to college, I did not think I could afford to. Another angel appeared. It was my high school assistant principal, who worked as adjunct faculty at a local nursing school, who started the conversation with my mother about college and financial aid. I thought I would give the idea a chance. I had always admired the role of news reporters that I had seen on television and had developed a strong interest in journalism and radio, but I knew I needed something immediately secure after I graduated. So, instead, I decided to become a nurse. I was able to graduate from high school a semester early. I started my first-part time job at a movie theater, and I began taking college prerequisites for nursing school. I returned at the end of the semester to walk at graduation with my senior class.

By my senior year, Mr. Wesley had introduced me to one of his former students, a young man a few years older than me whom he felt I could possibly share a nice courtship with. That young man was yet another angel in disguise. Little did I know that he would later choose to stand in the gap as the bridge to help me transition and grow through crucial stages of my life from college and beyond.

Unfortunately, by default, in addition to being a boyfriend, he ended up playing so many other roles, which should have been the responsibility of my father. So, the relationship was not perfect, but was divinely on purpose.

One of our dates included my timely introduction to a new church. It would be under the teachings of the pastor of that church that I learned about the power of words. It was Bishop Fred Caldwell who first taught me biblical scripture through life application. "Death and life are in the power of the tongue, and they that love it shall eat the fruit thereof" (Proverbs 18:21). The tongue as such a small part of the body (James 3:5), yet its use had the power of life and death according to the words we speak (Proverbs 18:21). This became a profound awareness for me. I learned to be careful with my mouth—to speak more positively. I also learned about the spiritual gifts uniquely embedded in all of us. I learned that the presence of God is *with* me, and that my unique divine gifts are very personal and *within* me.

It was such a relief in my understanding from preaching to actual teaching. I learned about grace and forgiveness, and that my salvation was permanent and could not be stripped away. What a relief it was for me! The atmosphere of the church was positive and uplifting, even though I had some of my family members who rejected it and called the church "a cult." Yet, I kept attending, learning, and growing. I was hungry and receptive to a new and more positive approach to my life. The principles that I learned at Greenwood Acres Full Gospel would be the strength that carried me throughout some of my darkest days, starting with college.

CHAPTER 10

WHEN TESTED, REMAIN TRUE

"Truth never damages a cause that is just."

—MAHATMA GANDHI

I was a terrible test taker and became anxious from the very moment an instructor would begin to simply hand out an exam. Multiple choice questions were the worst. True or false questions were always tricky. Presentations were much friendlier, and written essays and papers were where I did my best.

It was the toughest semester ever, and the one that mattered most. In a large class of nursing students, it would be determined who would finally be accepted into the long-awaited "clinicals." My name was nowhere on the list. I had not passed—once again. In total despair, I held back the tears. Feeling like such a failure, I sat and watched as my classmates one by one leaped for joy as the results came flooding in. Everyone around me was celebrating their victory. They were excited and making phone calls to their family and friends. They had accomplished a major goal of passing that final exam and making it to the next level. I saw classmates who had started with me in just one millisecond speed right past me. I felt left behind and afraid. Everyone was experiencing a win—except me. While they were excited and making plans to graduate, I slowly shrunk into nothingness. I wanted so badly to give up, but my very existence depended on it. I was overwhelmed and terribly exhausted. I felt unworthy and ashamed, but something within tugged at me to keep going.

And so, I did. I waited about a year before I was eligible and could successfully transfer from the local nursing school to another university out of state. I worked, took additional courses to pull up my grade-point average, and waited. I got a job as a substitute elementary school teacher to pre-K students. My interactions with those toddlers was the best therapy. The students ended up teaching me and were a part of my much-needed reassurance. They made me believe again. I felt worthy because I could actually help someone. I could teach. Meanwhile, I continued living at home with my mother. I thought a few times about forgetting nursing school and choosing a shorter route to be a nurse's aide, but a close friend encouraged me to keep pushing to earn my bachelor's degree. I knew I could not peacefully return to the school where I had failed and was nervous about having the resources to go off to college, especially to the private school I was hoping for. So, I prayed and asked for God's help. I kept working and applied to the school anyway.

My prayers were answered. A semester later, I was successfully living on a beautiful campus as a sophomore at East Texas Baptist University. Through financial aid, a student loan, scholarships, and grants that I didn't even know existed, I had the funding needed to go off to college.

It was my first time ever living away from home. I was blessed with kind and welcoming dorm mates, who over time became good sister friends. It was a healthy living space. I could focus, and I was affirmed. We encouraged each other through the difficult times. We were required to attend chapel regularly, and although it was a Christian-based university, the students were diverse and from various faiths and backgrounds. It was a beautiful glimpse from God.

This time, I studied even harder. Many nights my roommates headed to bed and wished me goodnight, only to greet me the next morning as I sat in the very same spot on the sofa as I burned the late-night oil. This was my grueling routine on alternate clinical days. While it seemed that everyone else was outdoors enjoying the sunshine, I was on the inside either catching up on sleep or studying. However, I became more confident and started to remember that I was smart. I knew that after all I had been through my first and second time around, there was no way possible that I would even come close to failing again. Yet and still, I had another downfall.

It was my senior year of nursing school and the trauma of taking exams would show up to haunt me once again. The paralyzing anxiety stuck its horrific tongue out at me, one final time! I started to panic. Weeks in advance before my last few exams, my anxiety became humungous leading up to those final days. I had two out of three exams remaining and still needed passing scores in order to graduate! To further throw a wrench in my anxiety came the odd scheduling of the pinning ceremony, which took place before the final exams. The pinning ceremony is a tradition to welcome new nurses into the nursing profession. Faculty members recognize each nurse in a formal service by presenting them with a nursing pin. Therefore, invitations had been sent out to my family and friends who were due to attend the service. I thought about how embarrassing it would be to participate in the pinning ceremony and in the next couple of weeks not be able to graduate! I dreaded the reality of that happening.

My classmates and I were required to have one-on-one meetings with our instructors to discuss whether we were in good standing going into the final exams before graduation. I became nervous. I knew that I had barely passed the multiple-choice portions of the exams that semester, but I thought that with my high scores on the clinical portion, I would yield a sufficient score. A passing grade was 80 percent; anything less was failing. I learned that day that my total score was 78.8 percent. I was three weeks away from my long-awaited graduation from nursing school. I had family and friends arriving two days later for my pinning ceremony, and yet I still had two remaining exams that were my only chance to bring up my final grade in order to successfully pass and graduate. What a nightmare.

I froze up. As my instructor said, "I am not sure what happens to the young lady that I see who does so well in the clinical setting, but when it comes to these exams you lose that confidence! I need that same smart nurse to show up in this classroom and put that information on paper, because you have demonstrated that you know this material! If you can't pull your grade up, you will not graduate!"

I couldn't say another word. In my dark state of disappointment, I walked back to my dorm, dropped my bags, and cried myself to the dorm room floor. My roommates had left for the weekend, and there I lay for hours in total disarray. Through my blinding tears, I saw the daylight through my window slowly turn into night, and from night back into day again. I had no appetite, no desire to talk to anyone, and nothing left—but one tiny prayer: *God, help.*

I somehow managed to rise to my knees to press play on my boom box. It was the soothing sound of Terry MacAlmon's live worship from the World Prayer Center that calmed me. And then I heard Jaci Velasquez singing "On My Knees." I listened and cried out to God. I asked for the one thing it was going to take for me to graduate—a miracle.

In my desperation I reached a place of total surrender, and for the first time ever I had a holy encounter. As I prayed and cried, a strong, tangible, vibratory force started to rise inside my belly. Its power vibrated from my stomach up to my vocal cords and came out of my mouth. The prayers that I was speaking in English suddenly transformed. The strength of my words was coming from my own heart, but the power guiding them became dual. I was not alone. Everything that I didn't have the power to pray in my English language was proceeded by a comforting presence in another language. I was filled with the divine gift of intercession—I was praying in spiritual tongues. The power inside of me literally manifested all around me and I was no longer afraid. My mind comprehended the loving utterance as it was clear that I only needed to believe. In that moment I was instilled with absolute trust that my needs would be met. I did not know how, but I believed that my needs would be met. The presence was word that had profoundly become life. My heart was reminded of the sacred scriptures: "The Advocate whom the Father will send will teach you all things and will bring all things to your remembrance" (John 14:26). "He will help you and be with you forever" (John 14:16). "He dwelleth with you and shall be in you" (John 14:17). It was the beginning of a new relationship, with the perfect new acquaintance. The holy one was closer than breath itself.

As I continued to pray, my tears of sadness became tears of joy. I was able to rise, clean myself up, and finally get to bed for what was the most peaceful and renewing sleep. I was able to rest because I had faith that I was going to make it. The power that was imparted to me reset my thoughts of impossibility into all possibility. I was at peace and felt restored.

I awoke the next afternoon and was prompted to go meet with my instructor, with no prearranged meeting, no formal appointment, and no clue of her schedule that day. My spirit was reassured that she somehow would be there. I got dressed and walked over to the nursing building within the same hour that afternoon. And there she sat in her office, as if she had been waiting for me all along. I walked in and spoke from a confidently new place. I shared with her my absolute truth. The truth that I had suffered from a horrific anxiety of test taking, and that I had struggled for years with the fear of failure before I'd even get an exam into my hands. I shared how I would study diligently until the knowledge became a part of me, but that the exams would somehow cripple me. I explained how I wished my tests could be in essay format with the option to freely write my responses, or that I could be allowed to verbally have question-and-answer sessions in which I could answer the test questions aloud versus having to panic in silence while selecting between multiple choices on paper.

My instructor gave me a long, hard stare, and for the first time, I saw empathy in her eyes as she replied, "We have dealt with this type of problem with some students before. It's called being too smart to be silenced, and your brain can't keep up with what your heart is trying to express! We are allowed to make special accommodations for super-smart students like yourself, you know. You need only do one thing." Startled, I answered "One thing?" She smiled and replied, "Yes! You need only ask. Ask, and it is given."

In total gratitude, I was delighted to learn that someone finally understood me, and that I had never been alone. With one conversation, a door had opened that led me to learn that a few of my fellow classmates also required special accommodations when it came to test taking. By the grace of God, the following week I was added to the group, and arrangements had been made so that we could each meet in a classroom one by one with a panel of nursing professors. Each test question was read aloud, and I was allowed to verbally give my answers. The next week, I received my final exam in written essay format. My prayers had been answered, and a miracle had occurred. I passed with flying colors.

Even when things go in the opposite direction from what you expected, do not sell yourself short. Stay true and speak up for yourself. Let truth be your intention because it ultimately prevails.

CHAPTER 11

GOOD WILL COME

"Inspiration comes from within yourself. One has to be positive. When you're positive, good things happen."

—DEEP ROY

Starting with my pinning ceremony leading up to my graduation, I received back-to-back victories in just a few short weeks. It seemed that ongoing miracles started happening for me. I could see the sun shining again. My hard work and prayers had paid off, and I realized that my journey was not in vain. I felt like I could do anything! I started to have job offers one after another. And once I secured my new nursing job that I was expected to start soon after I graduated, I took another leap of faith. While I still needed to pass my boards, I had decided early on that I really needed two things upon graduation: my own living space and quality transportation. So, I met with a wise and trusted friend who helped me plan how I could reasonably and responsibly establish an affordable life for myself as a new nurse. I learned of the many benefits that came with my new profession, including first-time graduate discounts from a variety of sources. In celebration of my graduation, I wanted to treat myself to something I needed, deserved, and had longed for—a new, reliable car. With proof of my graduate certificate, and no down payment, I was able to drive away on graduation day in my brand-new Toyota.

Immediately after graduation, I was also able to move into my first new apartment. I was scheduled to start my new job within a couple of weeks as a GN (graduate nurse), the status I would hold until I would receive proof of passing my boards as a RN (registered nurse). I had already taken prep courses a few months prior for my boards and had planned to take advantage of the time for more study. The strangest thing happened. In the silence of my apartment, as I gathered my reading materials, I was spiritually halted. It was the sweet familiar voice—my "inner counselor"—that instructed, "Relax."

Delighted and yet startled at the same time, I closed my eyes, paused, took a deep breath, and asked, "Are you saying that I should not study right now?" The faint voice lovingly replied, "You have no need. What I have given you is sufficient. The knowledge is already inside of you, so rest." I paused again, thinking that it was a bit unorthodox to have just finished nursing school and not even touch another prep manual before my boards! Needing further reassurance, I asked again, "So what are you saying?" The voice became a little louder as my spirit interpreted: "It is not necessary for you to study for your boards; you have the information inside of you already. Rest." In that very moment, as I sat in stillness with my eyes filled with tears, I could feel a deep comfort of love, care, and protection. The spirit whispered, "I *am* not of that which is tradition, and nor are you. Trust. I *am*."

And so, I surrendered. I trusted the voice. I felt relieved, as I had been given divine permission to take a much-needed break. I did not make any further plans; I did just as I was told. For the next two weeks, I relaxed. I took a lot of nature walks in the parks and trails along the south side of the Red River. I had very little communication with my loved ones at the time, as everyone thought I would be studying for my boards. I simply talked with God. I remember looking out onto the water, and with a spiritual ear I could hear God speak. "This my daughter, is mine, as are *you*! The birds flying in the air, the life of the water, the wind in the trees. There is no fear, no worry, and no need. I *am* your provider."

The morning arrived for me to take the National Council Licensure Examination for Registered Nurses (NCLEX-RN). I rose early in a rested state of gratitude and an incredible realization came to mind—I no longer had any test anxiety! I got dressed, drove to the peaceful riverfront where I had been communing with pure spirit. I gave thanks for His guidance, and I gave thanks in advance for the passing of my boards later that day. Thereafter, on to the testing site I drove. Joyfully and calmly, I walked in as a representative greeted me and said, "I have not seen any one walk into this place with a smile on their face until today!" "Thank you!" I replied. "Are you ready," he asked? "Oh yes, I am very ready!" I said. He gave instructions that there would be anywhere between seventy-five to 265 multiple choice questions depending on how well one is doing. I clearly understood the reputation of the NCLEX. It was a good sign if the exam stopped at the seventy-fifth question, and possibly not so good if the test continued for a lengthy 265. I sat down at the computer and gave thanks to God for the opportunity and for bringing me so far. For the first time in my life, question by question, I enjoyed taking a test. I read with easy comprehension and with little effort I recognized the best answer. I took my time, and after a couple of hours I arrived at my seventy-fifth multiple choice question. I gave thanks, submitted my answer, and just as I imagined—the exam shut off. Two weeks later I received confirmation in the mail of my passing scores with my certificate as a registered nurse.

I proceeded to start my career working on a medical-surgical unit. The journey was a full one, and I learned so much about myself in the midst of it all. I worked a few years in Louisiana before moving to Dallas to not only expand my career opportunities, but to also be closer to the man that I had hoped to marry. We loved each other and he had invested his time, energy, and resources into my personal and professional growth. He taught me so many valuable lessons and greatly influenced my decision to continue my education and complete graduate school. After several years of adjusting to the big-city life and working full time and additional per diem shifts at larger teaching hospitals, I decided to expand my potential by pursuing my graduate degree. For three and a half years, I committed to working three twelve-hour shifts from 7:00 a.m. to 7:00 p.m. Fridays, Saturdays, and Sundays in order to take graduate classes Monday through Thursday. It was a busy and challenging journey. I had my ups and downs and rewards running altogether. I bought my first new home, kept dating, fell deeper in love, and got my heart broken. I gained forty pounds, started practicing yoga, grew a head full of locs, and met a naturopathic doctor who would inspire the shift in my entire thought pattern surrounding the practice of traditional medicine. Upon completion of my master's degree, I was ready for something new.

CHAPTER 12

ALIGNING WITH THE DIVINE

"When you are in alignment with the desires of your heart, things have a way of working out."

—IYANLA VANZANT

The journey of my spiritual unfoldment began as I quit my job, loaded up my Toyota, left my beautiful and newly built home secured, and signed up to work as a travel nurse. I was no longer attached to anything or anybody. Material things mattered very little. I only wanted that which was real—the God stuff, the stuff built to last. On a path to self-discovery, I took my broken heart across the country from Texas to New Mexico, then Arizona to California. Taking on assignments in a variety of settings, I cared for patients in indigent rural areas and lived in small, modest cottages in the middle of nowhere. I later found myself working among highly affluent individuals in world-renowned medical centers such as Cedars Sinai in Beverly Hills. Still grounded in my faith, I had so many questions for God. I knew that I was simply different. My thinking was slowly shifting from the way I had been raised, the things I had been taught, and how I felt about life itself. I became a seeker of truth. And as the saying goes, "When the student is ready, the teacher will appear."

The small inner voice was the light guiding me. I was not moved by much. I wasn't impressed by the fame or any amount of fortune as I lived and worked in the middle of it all. I was led to a studio near my job directly on Sunset Boulevard in West Hollywood, where I ended up leasing from an actor who was working his way into the limelight. He left books and reading materials that I found myself scanning. Some of them I was already well acquainted with, and others were new. I was intrigued and curious. I started to receive divine "downloads." One step at a time, I trusted the inner voice, the one I could count on. In my search of purpose and fulfillment I needed answers from God that I had yet to find in the churches and religious settings I was previously a part of. I found peace in letting go more and more of that which no longer served me. I asked God to help me sift through the spiritual keepsakes and to toss out any falsehoods I was clinging to. I started to spend more time in nature, listening, praying, and communing with the Creator. The all-knowing spirit affirmed where I was going as I became fearless in my quest to visit various centers of different faiths. Synagogues, mosques, ashrams, temples, and sacred gardens seemed to hold a welcoming space for the courageous Christian who entered—me. Smiles, bows, prayerful mudras, nods, claps, handshakes, and warm embraces awaited me in every unique sanctuary.

I became a regular attendee on Monday nights at the Saban Theatre in Los Angeles, where I would go to hear Marianne Williamson's talk from a powerful blue book known as *A Course in Miracles*. Often, I was one of the few African Americans in an auditorium full of Jewish women and men. Without ever introducing myself, it was as if someone politely saved a seat for me every Monday night on the front row. And on Wednesday evenings and Sunday mornings, I found myself in the loving atmosphere of the Agape

International Spiritual Center, which was my weekly reprieve from the hustle and bustle of work.

Over time, as I prayed, I was led to more workshops, spiritual retreats, teachers, and thinkers alike who seemed to align well with the journey of my spiritual unfolding. My role and title mattered less as I started to transform in a way that I could see deeper parts of myself. I was more than a small-town girl with a broken heart. I was more than a nurse, more than the degrees I held, the jobs I worked, or the salary I earned. I was a child of an unconditionally loving God. A God who nurtured and comforted me like a mother, a God who protected and provided for me like a father, was the one who hand-picked me for a purpose.

I went on a ten-year hiatus from the local traditional church, taking the middleman out of the equation. I dove deeper into my boldness to ask questions of God Himself, questions that many only wondered about, or perhaps their culture or religion might frown upon if they even thought to explore. I started with simple questions: Who are You, God? Where did religion come from? Why are there so many to choose from? What is the truth? Through prayer and stillness, the answers started making their way into my consciousness. I was eventually given the peace of mind to take my traditional thoughts of God out of the box—bigger than the four walls of a building, bigger than the pages of one holy book. Beyond the voice or message of any preacher, religion, or belief system, it was simple. As nature would have it, just as there is one ocean with many waves, there is one God with many names. It was made clear to me that God's plan is unity—if only humanity adhered to it. God is not about division, and God is *not* a religion.

CHAPTER 13

FORGIVENESS FREES YOU

"Forgiveness is a gift you give yourself."

—TONY ROBBINS

My heart has been broken many times in my life in various ways. From the beginning, it was the abandonment and continued neglect of my father. Later came the emotional pain and resentment from my dear mother. As far back as I can remember I was hurt by my high school sweetheart, college sweetheart, and then simply by the agonizing search for the right sweetheart.

I spent years of my life not fully available for the romantic relationship I truly deserved because I held the space for someone who could never fully commit to me. The man I had loved for so long, who had become my best friend, had chosen someone else. It didn't matter if it was the wrong someone else, the fact remained—it wasn't me. I hoped and wished and waited for our timing to be just right, only to get a repeat of it being all so very wrong. He was a loyal friend, but a terrible romantic partner. It was so hard to understand how someone who had supported, encouraged, loved, and lifted me at the same time managed to break my very heart in two! It was a bitterly sweet chapter that over time I was finally able to release. It took years before I could fully move on. Hastily seeking an outlet for something that felt like love, I started attracting men who were already attached, and ended up doing something I wasn't proud of. I had an affair with a married man and found myself suffering alone and in silence after he was long gone. I quickly learned the tough lesson that the "forbidden fruit" of secret relationships amounted to nothing but a temporary thrill and emptiness in the end. I realized that I simply wanted to be chosen—but only by Mr. Right.

I prayed and eventually learned to forgive myself, and I knew that God forgave me too. Through reading materials, healing seminars, and spiritual counsel, I continued the process of forgiveness, extending it beyond myself and then to my best friend who had deeply hurt me. The healing thread of our relationship was the substance that had been there all along—an unconditional, indescribable *love*—the greatest formula on the planet. It heals all things. It brings about miracles. Even the kind where the person who broke your very heart might assist in its healing.

Over time, I sorted out the facts. We were two close friends who had essentially grown up with many similarities. Both of us had defied the odds of our upbringing and, over the years had found in each other what we both longed for: safety, acceptance, emotional availability, and love. It never meant that it would last forever, even though at the time I felt it would be. I realized God had a purpose for both of us in that journey. We taught each other. We helped each other grow. We loved hard. We hurt each other. We stopped speaking. We matured. We had our seasons of back and forth, and we finally blessed each other to move on. And thankfully, I was able to spiritually, physically, and emotionally clear my "man space" in order to make room for someone new.

I've been disappointed in my career numerous times. Being a young, ambitious, black woman, I took pride in representing my family and community in a way that many might not have believed possible. However, this would come only with faith, patience, and perseverance. I endured countless acts of subtle, and sometimes outright, discrimination and stereotyping throughout college and graduate school. Having these experiences while working so hard to earn my degrees were almost unbearable. It didn't end there. I would graduate into the real world of my profession, only to have some of those same unwelcoming experiences repeated! Nurses eating their young. White nurses ostracizing black nurses. Black nurses backbiting other black nurses. And the experience of meeting a white patient for the first time, and her instant demand for "another" nurse to care for her was beyond condescending to me. In the South, the predominant culture of black and white meant there was not a lot of diversity in my field, and unfortunately, in my travels I still did not have an ally in most of my environments.

Through it all, I remained hopeful. I prayed, affirmed, worked for, and believed in something better. For me, working as a bedside nurse was a good start, but I wanted to advance as a leader in the field, just as other nurses did. I showed up willing, with what I thought was all the right criteria to advance and climb the career ladder of the organizations in which I worked. However, this was not the case. My confidence and poise seemed to only draw out the ugly head and feelings of superiority (ego) and complexity that had infected the minds of many of those in leadership. I would show up for an interview excited, energized, and highly qualified for the promotion. Many times, I walked into a conference room full of people who didn't look like me (and some who did), only to observe them having to regroup as though the individual's resume that they were holding in their hands did not fit the image of the person in front of them. Time and time again, I was denied, overlooked, or outright disregarded for a promotion, only to witness a white or male counterpart who was often less qualified than I, receive the offer. After having worked and studied so hard, this was brutal for me. I eventually reached a peaceful point where I no longer desired "climbing" to those positions altogether. I became more purpose-driven and set a new intention to apply my focus toward that which I was created to do—which beautifully changed everything.

Each level of hurt that we experience will likely be different, but the reward of forgiveness is always the same: it frees you. As I learned this over the years, I was able to take a closer look at the pain stemming from my roots, starting with my mother's journey. A greater depth of empathy and understanding arose within me for her. And even though I am aware of the generational issues and complexities of my family, I discovered a deep well of overflowing grace and forgiveness for my mother.

Also, after many years, I was finally able to share with my father my feelings of disgust and disappointment in him. He listened, apologized, and owned up to his complete failure as a father. It was the most difficult act of forgiveness for me, and even though I chose to sever our contact, I wanted him to know that I forgave him too.

Through family dysfunction, broken relationships, racial discrimination, hostility in the workplace, and what appeared to be ongoing setbacks in my career, I have experienced pain on many levels. What did I learn from all of this? The power of compassion, humility, mercy, and forgiveness—there is a great global need for the expression of all of these. To live by such virtues, you will have a more free and healthier heart, allowing more love and less hate to be exchanged by you.

PART THREE

YOUR WAYS
(ACTIONS)

WHATEVER YOU PUT
OUT COMES BACK

CHAPTER 14

DO NO HARM
(NONMALEFICENCE)

"Make a habit of two things: to help;
or at least to do no harm."

—HIPPOCRATES

When I became a nurse, I took a pledge, and within the code of ethics was the first principle: Do no harm. I committed that I would not inflict intentional harm or injury to my patients and would take active measures to prevent it at all costs. However, I did not need to become a nurse to realize that any action that I take, be it positive or negative, has equal consequences. My life experiences and the morals held high within me is what has taught me this.

When we are children, a divine grace covers us until we know better, because in essence we are born good. Before parents and caregivers try to teach us their ways of right versus wrong, God embedded within our original DNA a purity and goodness that cannot be duplicated. We were created by love and are emanations of love. Therefore, our truest nature is to love. It is not natural to want to cause harm or suffering to someone. A desire to hurt someone without reasonable cause is not of God. This is learned behavior from society. Depending on one's upbringing, conditioning, morals, and values is what drives our behaviors. The consequences we receive are direct outcomes of our ways—the actions we take.

If there is any desire within you to cause pain or suffering to another group or individual, and you take the necessary actions to make sure it is so, then you have signed yourself up for an equal return on what you have invested. There is no getting around this. By the same law, when you commit acts of love, support, and kindness, the magnitude of that love will be returned in abundance to you! This sometimes occurs as a divine surprise when you least expect it. The people you were kind to may or may not be the individuals from whom your returned blessing comes.

In a world where hate, crime, lies, evil, and deception would seem to have made a lasting and final impression on us, please understand that there is a supernatural force within you to counteract it all. How do we do this?

It starts on an individual level. Regardless of what you have been taught, commit to doing good. It is simple as that. This does not mean for you to become a doormat and allow yourself to be taken advantage of. It means to be strong and intentional about applying your efforts toward grace and generosity. When you focus your gifts, time, talent, resources, and energy on creating more peace, joy, love, and positivity in this world, it becomes contagious.

Start with this affirmation: *Whatever I put out in the world is coming back to me, therefore I choose actions that are best for myself and the greater good of others. I will not cause intentional harm to myself or any other being. I was created by love; therefore, I am worthy to live, to give, and to receive love.* Now, take the initiative and act on it.

CHAPTER 15

YOU ARE MAGNETIC

*"If you want to find the secrets of the universe,
think in terms of energy, frequency and vibration."*

—NIKOLA TESLA

As a spiritual thinker, I have become very aware of the laws of nature that govern this universe. This means there are laws that were ordained by God, and no matter where you are on this planet, they apply. These laws do not require that you know the science— they *are* the science.

In an academic setting, these laws would be taught in the scientific discipline of physics or a branch of philosophy. For example, we cannot see electricity with the naked human eye. We can only recognize its effects on how it impacts other objects. A lightbulb is not electricity. It is the result of what electricity can do. Electricity provides light and power to the many appliances of our households, businesses, and industrial machinery. However, electricity existed before humans did, but it took humankind to evolve in order to discover its use.

As the ever-expanding good (God) would have it, scientists would later learn through the development of electroscopes and other sensitive instruments such as magnetometers that human beings are far more than flesh and bones. We carry our own electrical charges, both positive and negative. We have what is known as an "energy field" around each human body. Therefore, we are energy beings, and although with the naked eye we cannot see it, we literally vibrate! At all times, based on the actions we take, we are either emitting negative or positive vibrations (or vibes). Based on the interactions we have with others, we leave one's presence feeling either positive (expansive) or negative (constricted).

You can easily understand the energy field that surrounds each of us by envisioning a large circle around your entire body. Picture every person you encounter having an invisible circle surrounding them. Now imagine that the more peaceful thoughts you think, the more positive words you speak, the more love you put out, and the more life-giving nutritious food you eat, that circle to expand larger and brighter, encompassing others as you go about your day. When they catch the wave of your presence, they become happy and energized. Imagine walking by total strangers and them being uplifted without even understanding they came near such a high vibrational being. On the other hand, if you spend your time in low-frequency activities such as gossiping or having negative thought patterns such as fear and worry, and perhaps consuming too much junk food, you will carry the energy of a downer, or one who is of a depressed, sad, or unwelcoming nature. When others come around you, they leave quickly because the energy that you are putting out is of a low frequency. The only individuals who will want to stay in your presence are those of the same frequency. Consequently, whatever energy type you are consistently vibrating on, you will start to attract the same to yourself because your energy field is a spiritual magnet. Whatever your dominant frequency is, positive or negative, you will attract a matching vibration. Like attracts like.

This law of attraction applies to every friendship, family relationship, romantic relationship, business partnership, etc. It helps us clearly understand why people come and why they go. When you are aligned, it is easy and effortless. When you are no longer in sync, things become complicated. One of the best things we can do for ourselves is to make positive choices that keep us vibrating at a high frequency. Alternatively, we can be deliberate about staying clear of things and people that cause our frequency to be low.

You are more than just a human being; you are a magnetic force! Whatever choice you make at any given moment, you are deciding on what you will attract to yourself. Be wise in choosing how you vibe.

CHAPTER 16

NEWTON'S THIRD LAW

"It seemed a bit like an aura was leaving their bodies. Some brighter than others ... I want to live my life so my aura, when it leaves, is one of the brightest ones."

—JOHN DIAZ, a plane crash survivor

There is a spiritual boomerang that is always at work. It has been described in various ways throughout time, religiously, scientifically, and spiritually. Regardless of one's study, the formula does not change. The maker of all humankind knew that the uniqueness of each human being would require more than one explanation to align the different intellects, yet all reach the same goal. Therefore, numerous thinkers, teachers, creatives, leaders, and outliers would be born throughout history with the purpose of increasing our insight to accomplish one inclusive message: to love.

Historically, we were taught that Sir Isaac Newton, the legendary physicist and mathematician, discovered three simple, yet powerful laws. I suppose part of his purpose here was to bring to life a greater understanding of cause and effect or sowing and reaping. Newton played a vital role in introducing one of the early known and classical sciences: *mechanics*. Classical mechanics is the study of how bodies move by way of the natural laws of force. The study includes how gravity, electricity, and magnetism work. As the Creator would have it, Newton's passion for math and physics brought him to a place where he became the expert on three divinely orchestrated laws. Society would later deem these laws as "Newton's Laws of Motion" or the "Three Laws of Motion."

The first law (inertia) describes that when a thing or body is at rest, it will remain at rest unless an action of force comes to it. Likewise, if an object is in motion, it will remain in constant motion unless an external force halts it. Therefore, if a person or thing is not pushed or no force is applied, they tend to remain in a state of rest or complacency. Once you are in motion, you keep moving forward unless a force outside of you causes you to stop. This law also affirms that any force of friction hinders an object. Even when an object is in steady, constant motion, when friction arises, it will be slowed and eventually come to a complete stop.

The second law (mass and acceleration) describes the quality of impact that a force has on an object—its momentum. The level of force applied determines the magnitude, direction, and time rate in which an object will change. If you are highly influenced by an external source of great magnitude, you will change the course of your direction very quickly. If you are influenced by a weaker force, with lesser impact, you will make changes at a slower rate. Your momentum is impacted by the magnitude of which the force occurs.

The third law of motion, which is my primary focus point, proves that when we apply a specific force to an object, the force will equally return in the opposite direction from which it was sent. Meaning, whatever you put out and the force that you exert behind it will equally be returned to you. It does not matter who you are, what you have or do not have, or what status you have reached on society's scale of status. Whatever you sow in this earthly realm, you will also reap. Your soul knows. This is God's universal law.

CHAPTER 17

THE GOLDEN RULE

*"Therefore all things whatsoever ye would that
men should do to you, do ye even so to them:
for this is the law and the prophets."*

—MATTHEW 7:12

One principle that is pure gold crosses many religions and sacred texts. Why gold? Because its value is of the highest ethical quality, respect, and care. It is none other than the Golden Rule: *"Do unto others as you would have them do unto you."* It summarizes the greatest intention we should all have toward one another.

Do not do anything to anyone that you would not want done to yourself. It is that simple. If you can follow this one rule, an improvement in your overall well-being becomes the byproduct. Did you know that when you do good to others, certain "feel good" hormones (endorphins, serotonin, and dopamine) are released in your brain? These hormones cause a feeling of optimism and satisfaction that runs throughout your entire body! Do you ever wonder why when you give to a total stranger or someone in need, your spirits as well as the other person's are instantly lifted? This is because on a soulful level, you have activated your worth—and theirs. Human kindness helps heal us all. This also applies to the workplace. Whatever industry you serve in, if you can make a conscious decision to treat your coworkers the way that you would like to be treated, such a positive attitude will work in your favor and go a long way. Also, showing up and doing the job that you have been hired to do to the best of your ability gets you to the next level. That next level may or may not be within the organization where you sowed your good seeds, but because divine compensation is always at work, life will be sure to elevate you.

I would also like to add a parallel to this golden principle: treat yourself as you would want others to treat you. I endorse self-love! It not only raises your vibration, but keeps your frequency high, causing you to attract greater love to yourself. It also teaches others how to treat you. Life will mirror back to you how you treat yourself, by giving you more of the same experiences based on what you have demonstrated as your value. This equates to how you carry yourself: your entire body temple and your personal hygiene, including the cleanliness of your hair, your teeth, your skin, your hands, your feet, etc. Treating yourself like the king or queen that you are affirms your majesty. The commonly expressed proverb, "Cleanliness is next to godliness" holds true. How you treat yourself (and others) on the outside reveals the *glory* residing on the inside.

CHAPTER 18

DEFY NEGATIVITY IN THOUGHTS, WORDS, DEEDS, AND CONSUMPTION

"By thought, the thing you want is brought to you. By action, you receive it."

—WALLACE D. WATTLES

If you can shift your thoughts, your words, and your actions in a positive direction, you will undoubtedly be a blessing to this world. If you live from a negative state, you will curse it.

Whatever you think, say, do, eat, drink, and give your brain power to becomes a seed at that very moment. Be it positive or negative, you plant a seed. Seeds have great potential to multiply and become stronger. If you surround yourself with positivity, you will attract more of it. If you spend most of your time in negative environments, you will draw more negativity to you. Sow your time and energy wisely. Your brain is fertile ground. Whatever you allow to enter on a regular basis will expand.

No matter where I am in my daily travels, there are what I call "phone zombies" among us. People are walking, running, driving, working, and operating machinery all while their eyes are glued to their cell phones. Of the many years since social media became a thing, I purposely never took part until recently. And even now, I joined with one intention in mind: to positively sow and reap from the good of it. I am very disciplined in filtering and limiting my use, and this practice has served my mind so well. Stepping away from our phones, televisions, and electronics for extended periods keeps us humane and connected in natural ways that the "wires" do not. In a world where mental health has become a major concern, I recommend unplugging and spending as much time in nature as possible. The God-given elements provided by Mother Nature promote health and healing like nothing else. Sunshine, water, air, rest, exercise, whole foods, nutrition, physical touch, and interaction with loved ones all play a vital part in our total health.

One of the healthiest detoxes you can give to yourself is to rid yourself of people, things, and environments that do not align with your highest good. For some, this may mean removing yourself from a toxic relationship or work setting that totally drains you. For others, this may involve limiting your intake of television and social media or eliminating gossip and negative conversations. This could also include doing away with low-frequency foods such as fast foods, junk food, or sodas for your health's sake. It takes wisdom to recognize when something no longer serves you. It is critical to know when a season has come to an end. This could involve a long-standing friendship that you previously thought would always be. Every relationship is not meant to last a lifetime. Some are only seasonal, which can be a very difficult reality. Conflict arises when we "extend our stay" beyond what is divinely intended. Also, some relationships of your bloodline or the family you were born into may not be meant to be a part of your future. Some people are simply teachers, to help you learn a particular lesson. Others are meant to help you get to your next level, and once the assignment is completed, something happens to conclude the relationship. The problem is many may not want to acknowledge when that end has come. However, when you are brave enough to surrender and let go, life has a way of assisting you. Once you release what no longer is good for you, you will always receive something special and new.

.

CHAPTER 19

SPEAK AND SHOW GRATITUDE

"How people treat you is their karma; how you react is yours."

—DR. WAYNE DYER

The ability to say *thank you* is one of the best kept secrets to attract more abundance to yourself. The energy of gratitude raises your vibration to a very high level! Do less complaining and more thanksgiving. From the moment you rise in the morning and as you go about your day, find reasons to be grateful. From your breath itself, to the safety of your sleep, to your ability to be oriented in your rightful mind, give thanks. There are a multitude of blessings that are often taken for granted, such as your ability to see, hear, taste, touch, and smell. Give thanks to God for all things and for the people who make a difference in your life. Show that you appreciate who they are and what they bring. This practice alone will draw more positive experiences to you.

I believe the spirit of gratitude is not just a verbal "thank you," but also a particular attitude that follows and shows just how grateful you truly are! It radiates from the inside out, and when you do not sincerely appreciate someone, they know it. There are many times that I have gone above and beyond to show support, kindness, and love, only to receive a mediocre thanks or no appreciation at all. We should not do things to necessarily get something in return, but the response and attitude that you get back is a good indicator of the heart of the receiver. Thankfulness should be a natural response; however, this is not always the case. Lack of gratitude can disrupt or even destroy relationships. After showing up fully and authentically in the name of love, friendship, family, etc., we still must preserve ourselves. We must make sure our own cup is full before pouring out of it. Taking care of ourselves is a top priority of gratitude. The well-being of our bodies, our hearts, our minds, and our peace is a daily responsibility. To be a good steward with what you already have is gratitude in action. It tells the Creator that you can handle receiving more.

I know what it is like to be taken for granted and to be taken advantage of. Therefore, gratitude is a way of life for me. I learned to set healthy boundaries or disconnect completely from those who do not honor and respect the value that I bring. And I strive to always do my part to speak and show my appreciation to those who are in some way, big or small, there for me.

The formula for gratitude is easy. When you receive, give thanks. When you give to others, give thanks for your ability to give. Give thanks for what you currently have and give thanks in advance for what you believe you will receive. Blessings are always in constant flow, so we are always receiving. Keep an attitude of appreciation for what is now and what is to come. Do this daily and you will find yourself having more and more to be grateful for.

CHAPTER 20

LISTEN TO THE SMALL VOICE

*"And thine ears shall hear a voice behind
thee, saying, this is the way."*

—ISAIAH 30:21

We all have an inner navigational system. Depending on our God-gifts and how we live our lives, some have a more heightened awareness than others. I believe that our gifts can show up in their best form when we are healthy and functioning at a high level versus having a gift and not being able to maximize its use due to bad habits or an unhealthy lifestyle. I have known since I was a child that I was blessed with something different. Although I could not form into words what I had been given, I knew that I could somehow discern what people near me were feeling and sometimes thinking. At first, I thought it was a normal thing for everyone until the gift started to grow. As I grew, it expanded from my ability to see the heart of a person, to having a keen insight when radical events were about to occur. I did not know the right words to explain how I was able to sense or "see" things and the different ways the gift would manifest. I never spoke about it, until friends, colleagues, patients, and total strangers started to confirm it. When I learned to meditate, get more still, and changed the foods I was consuming, the downloads started to come with greater clarity. It seemed that I had developed a keener awareness with some sort of telepathic ability, premonitions, dreams, and foresight.

The small voice within me would reach high amplitudes and my discernment grew stronger and louder. When the gift is activated, like prayer, the physical distance between me and another does not matter. An intense "knowing" overtakes me. As a nurse, I realized this was a perfect gift to have, especially with infants or adult patients who could not speak due to medical reasons. It gave me an advanced understanding of what they were experiencing and how best to care for them. At times, I felt so connected that even if I had stepped away from their room, I could "feel the call" for help before I was even notified on the call light. This gift has also served well in detecting when something about their treatment was going wrong.

Having such sensitivity at times seems like a blessing and a curse. Some things revealed are just difficult to accept and can be overwhelming. I had to learn that I am not meant to share all that I "hear" or "see," but I have known that however I use it, it must be applied with good intentions and for the betterment in each unique situation.

While on a quest to learn more about the holistic side of health and complementary medicine, I had some experiences that were good and some that were frightening. In those moments, even then the small voice, which became louder, gave reassurance that I was going to be OK. For this reason, the "inner knowing" has been my holy guide. It gives warning and serves as a protective agent when I need it most.

One of those times was a late winter afternoon in a smoke-filled room of burning sage, as I lay on a quilted massage table for what I believed to be a sound healing session with a professional sound practitioner. The moment my eyes were covered with blindfolds, I knew I was in trouble. As tuning forks were placed in each of my hands, and a blanket over my feet, I felt trapped as if invisible chains had paralyzed me to the table. I felt the wind of the so-called sound healer as she slowly strutted circles around me singing, chanting, and laughing in a shifty tone. She paused and attempted to guide me through a mysterious story line of deceptive conditioning. With my eyes still covered, a heavier scent of what was no longer sage began to smell like burning flesh. I immediately discerned wickedness.

My spirit was quickened, and a familiar vibration arose uncontrollably inside my belly! And while she continued to try to captivate a spell, the spirit within me was activated and out of my mouth came prayers in spiritual tongues! Every living and moving thing around me heard this divine command, from the chirping birds to the silent butterflies—and the disguised sound healer whose work was really witchcraft!

She had publicly presented herself as an experienced professional of the healing and musical arts, however, in private, out came the truth of her practice of darkness. She had a beautiful singing voice, yet also a twisted soul with a fetish for mind games and dark magic.

In that moment, I could feel the presence of my great-grandmother, who had passed on years before. As she placed what seemed to be a warm shield around me, and I was reassured of my safety. As I quickly rose off the table and removed the covers from my eyes, the holy authority inside of me arose with me. I was suddenly filled with a powerful peace. The scheming artist trembled as she heard the tongues uttering out of my mouth. She stopped everything and took a big step backward! Shaken, she said, "The spirit that is within you is very strong, like a force that is rejecting this for you! Which way do you wish to leave? You can use whatever exit you like!" I grabbed my shoes and headed out the door with a friend who had accompanied me and was waiting for me to complete the appointment. After leaving, I was guided to rid myself of all the clothing that I wore in that space, drink lots of water, and to make a visit to Whole Foods Market to pick up some fresh produce to prepare a healing meal. I prayed with my friend, and we affirmed the power, protection, and correction of God over our lives. I knew that my prayers had immediately counteracted the evil encounter that had taken place that afternoon. The "inner guide" yields comfort, reassurance, and security on a supernatural level, when necessary.

Another incident occurred on a dark winter night while I was visiting Costa Rica. In the middle of the Costa Rican jungle, I wept as I found myself among total strangers who were dazed and drunken. What started out as a plant-based medicine ceremony turned out to be a whirlwind of confusion and chaos. With a group of fellow tourists, I stood to meet the long-awaited shaman who was known as a gifted medicine man who had helped many heal from various diseases and dysfunctions of the mind and body by use of an herbal plant brew and other healing modalities. I had done about as much research as I could on the therapy and was interested in its effect as a natural preventive medicine. However, on this particular night, the guru was not present, and another group of novice shamans had been designated to administer the treatment known as *ayahuasca*. The trust and reputation of the leader caused a sense of safety for the attendees. Even though he was not present, the assigned shamans might offer the same medicinal benefit. Therefore, as candles were lit and music resounded, one by one, each participant proceeded to partake of the thick, muddy-tasting herbal liquid, which was administered in a shot glass.

I received a "hunch" inside of me and became uneasy as I was next in line. Regretfully, I quickly tilted back my head with one big gulp and swallowed the grainy liquid. I immediately felt that something was not quite right about the formula. I had moved one minute passed the *voice* alarming me. So, I started to pray as I began to feel dizzy and faint. I immediately called for help —God's help. I prayed for the safety of my mind, and that God would allow my body to become desensitized to the solution that I had just drank. Instantly, I felt my stomach as it started to reject the solution. I quickly made my way to the restroom. Miles away from my casita, I was not scheduled for pickup until several hours later. We were informed that the healing ceremony would last for several hours.

I had no cell phone reception, no transportation, and no light except candles and the stars in the sky. Tears rolled down my face. I was scared and disappointed as I sat and watched the spiraling behavior of those around me fainting and howling while grunting and vomiting. Then came the spontaneous rushing of several unidentifiable animals in the dark, running through the jungle making their way in and out of the *maloca* where we were. My heart raced as tears poured. I was thousands of miles, oceans, and airplane rides away from home. Holding tightly to my meditation pillow, I could only trust what was the most palpable presence that brought warmth and perfect peace—the hand of the Almighty. I wept as my mind recalled an earlier voice of my former pastor, Bishop Caldwell, who years before recited the sacred scripture in Luke 10:19. "Behold, I give unto you power to tread upon serpents and scorpions, and over all the power of the enemy, and nothing shall by any means hurt you." I continued to weep, as my spirit also heard the voice of an elder friend, Eula Pier, who had passed on years prior. She reminded me just as she always would, saying, "The perfect love of God cast out all fear." My tears then turned into peace and joy. I was comforted as I waited to be picked up and safely returned to my casita.

Through my travels, that inner voice has been with me. I stay attuned to it, and it always leads me to peace and safety.

PART FOUR

YOUR WISDOM (INSIGHT)

YOUR PLATFORM IS ON DIVINE DISPLAY

CHAPTER 21

LIGHTS, CAMERA, ACTION

"All the world's a stage."

—WILLIAM SHAKESPEARE

The divine director shines His marvelous light, keenly zooms in on the cosmic camera, then outwardly reveals your course of action, which determines the final take. Are you ready?

There is a wisdom code inside you of the truth you should be living. What you know and how you use it determines the destiny of your soul. It does not matter where your place is on the hierarchy of societal status. Regardless of where you live, work, do business, or your role or occupation—big or small, seen or behind the scenes—you have a platform, and God is always watching.

At any given moment, whatever role you play in this life is your stage. It is the platform given to you on your life path by God. Do not settle for the thought that you are doing whatever it is by chance. That role, that position, that occupation, that service, that detour, that downfall, etc. led you to something or someone. Coincidences do not exist. Pay attention to your platform and whatever audience that you serve, because it all has a purpose. Don't misuse or abuse it. While there are numerous roles, titles, and occupations in this world that are worthy of applause and accolades, a handful seem to have the most pressing duty and greatest impact for the healing of humanity.

CHAPTER 22

FOR PARENTS AND GRANDPARENTS

*"When my father and my mother forsake me,
then the Lord will take care of me."*

—PSALM 27:10

I f you place a beautiful plant or bouquet of flowers in an area that
has part sun and part shade, the flowers will naturally lean in the
direction of the sunlight. Seeds always grow toward the light.

Parents, your children are your seeds. Be sure that you are a
light that shines bright in their lives. They will more easily lean in
the direction of your radiance versus that which is dark or gloom.

Light represents peace, love, safety, gentleness, nurturing, honesty,
and accountability. Children need this more than ever. The opposite
of light is darkness, which represents pain—that which is unloving,
neglectful, harsh, rude, coldhearted, dishonest, and irresponsible. It
is your responsibility to dispel the negatives. Be careful that you do
not impose your past or your pain upon your children. Wisdom is
the knowledge gained from your life experiences.

For the many parents of this world who have been hurt or *are* hurting, know that your wounds are your wisdom. If someone hurt you when you were a child, the wisdom of that experience gives you the opportunity to be careful that your own child is protected in a way that neither you nor anyone else will hurt them. It does not mean that you will always be able to prevent harm, but it does mean that you honor their lives as precious and purposeful while doing your best to maintain their security. As parents and grandparents, if you can view the life of your child as a gift or seed from God, you can keep your intentions good. If you view them as a curse or an inconvenience, you may begrudgingly treat them unfairly or resent them without realizing it. They will feel and know the difference.

Know that if these miraculous beings made it safely out of the womb and into this world, they were meant to be here, regardless of the journey leading to their arrival, and you were the vessels to bring them.

Before coming into their own state of awareness, children often mirror the attitudes and behaviors of their parents. Therefore, parents are the primary leaders who set the tone for the future of this world. Each generation represents a newer version of what came and went before. If the proper seeds are planted and carefully nourished, the offspring can more easily blossom.

Not only is it important to protect the well-being of your children, but also your own. I personally know this, having been a seed that marinated in the womb of a young teen who by default had to become a brave single mother. While trying to save herself, she had to do everything possible to ensure that I was also safe. I clearly understand that this was no easy feat, but she persevered to figure out a better path for both of us. I am forever grateful for the bold journey my mother took to ensure that I was protected to the best of her will and wisdom.

We are all seeds from the journey of our parents and grandparents. We can learn valuable lessons from their lives about how best to leave a mark of our own. A trademark is a recognizable imprint from an original design that ensures the product or brand is protected. Parents, children are divinely trademarked to you, as products of God. It is your responsibility to love, nurture, support, and protect them to the best of your ability—body, mind, and spirit. And when you have done all that you can do, God will take it from there.

Dear God,

Thank You for the parents and grandparents of this world, who birth and bring forth all human life.

I understand that the responsibility is mighty, and many fall short of this charge.

May the parents of this world take heed to the blessings they have been given called children.

Activate Your power within them, that they may lead from a place of divine instruction.

May the wounds of our parents be well, so that they may love from a healed versus a broken heart.

Grant them the wisdom to see themselves and their children as gloriously as You see them.

May the platforms called parenthood align with Your miraculous love.

And so it is, Amen.

CHAPTER 23

FOR TEACHERS, PROFESSORS, AND LEADERS IN EDUCATION

"No one should teach who is not in love with teaching."

—MARGARET E. SANGSTER

The platform of a classroom comes with a doorway to many vulnerable hearts and minds. When you are in a position to teach, treat the students as you would want to be treated yourselves. You must recognize that you have faces from unknown places, with experiences that you may never understand. Each pupil has a story. Some have a tough narrative from the time they wake up through everything they had to do just to get to school.

From my pre-K years as a toddler to graduate school as an adult, being a product of the public and private school systems made me realize that teachers and professors must have awareness of themselves and others. This includes social and cultural competence and sensitivity.

I recall the situation of a child who had several siblings and a hardworking single parent. They had very few clothes and had to share mostly everything, right down to their underwear. That kid would rush to school just to make sure breakfast was a guarantee. Dinner was not promised, and at times for their family it was nothing more than scraps. Imagine the stress of having to think about food or clean clothing while having to struggle to study and complete homework.

Another scenario was a set of children who came from a "perfect" family from the outside looking in. But when they were left alone with their stepfather, he inappropriately touched and molested them. The children were well-dressed and wore what seemed to be permanent smiles on their faces. The hidden truth was they had to show up every day at school after being abused and violated, and they were afraid to return home each day. They had been groomed to be happy and "keep a secret," which was a heavy burden to bear. It wasn't until one of the children felt comfortable enough to finally confide in their favorite teacher that the abuse was stopped. That teacher completed the necessary protocol of mandatory reporting to start an investigation, and with the involvement of child protective services, the children were brought to safety and their stepfather was eventually arrested. It is actions such as this that turn teachers and educators into superheroes.

I mention these incidences because numerous stories like these happen across all age groups. The classroom brings with it busy minds that carry what is sometimes difficult to fathom. Therefore, a one-size-fits-all approach may not be the best method while trying to educate them.

Teachers, professors, and leaders in education are superheroes who can uniquely activate their magical powers when students need it most. Using the heart versus the head in some instances can create the greatest impact and make a lasting impression for a lifetime. Let your intentions be positive and pure. Empathize with the students. Do your best to keep them safe. Stay current and culturally competent. Give grace when necessary. Leave any personal biases on the other side of the classroom door. Check yourself and do it often. Assess what improvements you can make for the betterment of all. Take care of yourself. Set an intention to show up and deliver from the healthiest, most holistic state possible on the stage you have been given to serve—within and outside the classroom.

Dear God,

Bless the teachers and educators of this world.
Guide their interactions with each student.

May their classrooms and offices serve as safe havens
to extend their listening ears and rightful
wisdom to each student's heart.

May the truth emerge in their lessons, and wherever necessary,
allow Your higher consciousness to intervene
to correct any falsehoods.

Protect the teachers and protect the students.
May they each find and align with their highest life purpose.

And so it is, Amen.

CHAPTER 24

FOR DOCTORS, NURSES, AND HEALTH-CARE WORKERS

"Take responsibility for the energy that you bring."

—JILL BOLTE TAYLOR

The duty to safely hold the life of someone else in your own hands is one of great responsibility. To be a part of such a profession has allowed me firsthand knowledge and exposure to the care and complexities required to uphold it.

As doctors, nurses, and health-care workers, the best thing we can do for the patients and families that we serve is to treat them all with the same dignity, respect, and care. There can be nothing less, regardless of if they have less, come from less, or are labeled or stereotyped by society as *less*. No one should be treated any less than we want to be treated ourselves. We must practice and maintain this with our patients—and each other.

One of the things that I admire most about physicians is the mutual respect and camaraderie they have. It does not matter whether they are in each other's physical presence. Be it in person, in writing, on the phone, local or long-distance, the physician-to-physician comradeship is consistent.

Many times, have I experienced a physician or resident see me on an elevator or in the hallway of a hospital when I'm wearing my white lab coat. I notice that before they even speak, they take a glance at my badge or my embroidered credentials (RN, MSN) just to ensure they are not "overlooking" one of their very own. Most times they will proceed without speaking or initiating small talk once they are close enough to realize that the credentials on my white lab coat do not show MD. Physicians are deliberate about greeting each other and getting along. Many who work in health care observe this and understand just how strong the physician code is.

Unfortunately, from my experience, this is not the case in the culture of nursing. As frontline workers, the energy that it takes to perform high-quality patient care should not be minimized by cliques, hostility, competitiveness, backbiting, or personal conflicts. Such behaviors cause a negative transfer of energy from the caregiver to the patient and carries such a low frequency. The intention of any health-care facility is to be a healing space to improve the health and recovery of individuals and families. The intention of the health-care worker should be the same, starting with ourselves.

I recommend making self-care a top priority. Take care that you are well first—mentally, physically, and spiritually—before sharing your energy field with others, especially those who are sick and vulnerable and need your help, but also with your colleagues who are there to help you get it all done. You never know when it might be your turn to become a patient. You would then have sown the seeds full circle for a healthy return.

On the last day of my final class before completing my master's degree at the University of Texas at Arlington, my professor, Dr. Sharon Judkins, said to us, "Take a good look around this classroom. When you leave this campus and go out into the world, remember these faces that you have studied, cried, and conquered with … and when you are in position to do so, scratch each other's back and look

out for one another, as fellow nurses and friends." How nice would
that be?

Dear God,
May the healers be healed
so that they can more greatly relieve the suffering of this world.
Allow those who need You to find You.
Help them to recognize that some of their
patients are angels in disguise.
Fill their hearts with unconditional love.
Show them miracles, so that they might believe.
And so it is, Amen.

CHAPTER 25

FOR MINISTERS AND SPIRITUAL LEADERS

*"It is high time for thy ministers, O God, to
lift up their voices like a trumpet."*

—GEORGE WHITEFIELD

Men and women of the cloth, if you are serving in spiritual
leadership, your mandate is high. Your platform either binds
the captives or sets them free.

Whether you call God Yahweh, Allah, Elohim, Jehovah,
or Brahman, what matters most is that your message is leading
humanity to love.

The world needs individuals and communities with a
wholehearted mission to bring the light. Lightworkers walk in their
truth, freedom, and birthright given by God. Their intentions are
for the good of *all* humankind. Their actions are driven by their
divine inner wisdom, and they serve as beacons of hope and healing.

Ministers and spiritual leaders can play a pertinent role in the
mental, emotional, and spiritual well-being of the planet. When love

is the mission, there is no need to compare, compete, or contend about religion. We are all interconnected and came from the same source.

The greatest new intention that we could all have is to attain God's wisdom on how best to stay prepared for the now, and more so, what is to come in our ever-evolving world. Regardless of your religion or faith, more than ever before, we need you to stand together in love. It is the greatest force!

Believe and know that the Creator, our mighty ancestors, spiritual guides, and teachers are always with us and readily available to help when trouble rises against us.

Dear God,

May the ministers and spiritual leaders of this world
arise as bold beacons in a society filled with fear.

Provide them with Your staff and shield
for what is, and what is to come.

Protect them as they walk in Your power,
in service as lightworkers to Your people.

Give them Your mind, think through them.
Be their intuition.

Refresh their sanctuaries
with the spirit of love and truth.
And so it is, Amen.

CHAPTER 26

FOR THOSE OF HIGH RANK AND IN POSITIONS OF AUTHORITY

"To whom much is given, much will be required."

—LUKE 12:48

Those in positions that make the most influential decisions carry a heavy weight. In essence, you have been given the privilege to "play" God or to perform the *character* thereof. In some aspect of humanity, your authority could likely cause great impact on the masses. Therefore, you have the potential to either make or break the livelihood of others. In everyday life, making the right decision for ourselves alone can be a challenge, especially if we are not grounded or do not know how to tap into the power within us. However, we can improve our decision-making abilities through use of spiritual technologies such as stillness, prayer, and meditation. We can call upon our higher power to assist us in making the next best move. To serve in a high-ranking role must be even more difficult, because you have to decide on the outcomes or best-case scenarios for the people or the communities that you serve. Nonetheless, God is available to you, too.

The evidence of God and goodwill is reflected in how we treat ourselves and how we treat others. Spiritually and metaphysically, the two are never separate; they go hand in hand. We cannot treat ourselves well yet treat others poorly, or do good toward others yet put ourselves on the back burner. One will always impact the other. We must have a healthy balance in order to thrive well. We cannot be only *for* ourselves and expect the rest of the world to revolve around us, which aligns with selfishness. Nor can we give our best to others yet give the very least to ourselves, which indicates self-neglect or lack of self-love. So how can you do both—show up in the world at your best, while serving for the good of all, from a spirit "of power, and of love and of a sound mind" (2 Timothy 1:7)?

It all starts with desire. We must first have a desire to bring goodwill to all beings. If this is not the intention, then the world becomes corrupt, and the Creator must intervene. If you are in a position of high authority and your influence is great, use your platform to serve the people, as if you were serving God Himself, because in essence, you are. Be a voice for the voiceless, because the voiceless belong to God. And when it is in your hand to do so, have mercy as you would want mercy to be granted to you.

The great law of life gives the final verdict for our actions here on earth. When you conclude your time in the flesh and transition back to spirit, you want to ensure that your soul approves. How do you do this? By using your platform from the very top to the very bottom, in service of God and love!

Dear God,
May the leaders of this world remember their origin
And that the truest salvation can only come through You,
the alpha and omega.
May the hearts and souls of this planet
be led to Your everlasting truth and
healed by an agreement of love.
And so it is, Amen.

PART FIVE

YOUR WIN
(YOUR WORLD)

BE THE RISING TIDE

CHAPTER 27

CITIZENS OF THE UNIVERSE

"I live in a loving, abundant, harmonious universe, and I am grateful."

—LOUISE HAY

When the Creator blasted beautiful humans onto the evolutionary scene, purpose was the spark, and love was the flame!

We belong to God, and the *universe* is our "welcome home" agent. It is moral. It is friendly. It is inviting. It summons us to gather, to grow, to harvest, to share. It is far beyond the physical; it is energetic, intellectual, and spiritual. It offers the grandest experience of a lifetime, from spirit to flesh and flesh back to spirit! It is divine intellect. It co-creates with our thoughts, words, affirmations, faith, and belief systems. It supports us in becoming the greatest version of ourselves, but there is one agreement: it only responds with a yes to whatever you demonstrate that you wish. Note the word *demonstrate*, which is a clear expression of your faith and feelings in action. Your feelings, be they good or bad, happy or sad, will be multiplied according to whichever you feel most often. Therefore, it is important to do things and surround yourself with people who make you feel your best!

The universe is a yes personality. Its language is energy, frequency, vibration, and love. Whatever you put out more of, or feel more of, translates to what you want more of—whether positive or negative. The universe's response is yes. For example, if you constantly speak and think of lack, doubt, worry, or fear, it will assume you want more of it, and your frequency will be interpreted as: "I want more opportunities to experience lack, doubt, worry, and fear." The more time you spend thinking those thoughts and feeling those negative emotions, the more negative your vibration. However, if you speak, think, and find ways to *feel* abundance, better health, peace, joy, and love, you will experience plenitude. Some use vision boards (i.e., placing pictures or images of things that you desire on a board in your home or office, so you can always refer to it), or visioning (taking time out each day to be still and visualize what you want and feel it as if it is happening for you now). Many choose uplifting music with lyrics to support envisioning their dreams and boosting their "feel good" moments. Learning to meditate also highly supports our connection to the divine. There are many tools to bring about happy feelings to raise our vibrations and keep us uplifted versus feeling low. Remember, whichever frequency you choose—good or bad, high or low—the universe will mirror it back to you. Use the wisdom of knowing this to adjust your life where necessary. The energy of your intentions, actions, and reactions will always be supported. It is spiritual law.

The universe is also an advocate for love. It provides ongoing opportunities for us to love despite our differences and gives the reality check that no matter what, we are all interconnected. Every human on this planet is connected to the next. We are all masterpieces of the most high.

When things get tough, please remember that you are a miraculous being and you are never alone. Your neighbors and friends across the globe are having the same human experience. Expand your idea of "home" beyond the street that you grew up on, the city or state from which you are from, and the country where you were born. We are all interconnected and have a universal citizenship. Within you lies the power to conquer and overcome whatever may happen in this life. You were born with God's dream embedded inside of you! When you are in any situation where you are made to feel unwelcome, remember that you are in this world but not of it. Your home is where God is. And God is wherever you are—living, moving, and being throughout this entire universe.

CHAPTER 28

LIVE YOUR TRUTH

"The world needs that special gift that only you have."

—MARIE FORLEO

No matter what anyone says or thinks, we must understand that when we are functioning from our truest personality, it is then that it becomes the perfect match for our soul! To be yourself is what the great "I am" within you intended. Nothing more, nothing less.

We live in a society where you can change your image in a matter of minutes or even seconds. And we were all born with free will and have the choice to do so. However, the true you is what resides on the inside: your persona, your character traits, your identity, and your distinct qualities. Your original makeup is what makes you *who* you are. Living in a world where television and social media can have a heavy impact on our mental, emotional, physical, and spiritual well-being, we must stay grounded in our truth!

In order to do this, we must unapologetically be willing to turn off and turn away from any person or thing that causes us to question our worth. From the way we look (our hair, skin, body type, etc.) to the gifts and talents we each uniquely bring, we cannot live peacefully if we compare ourselves to others. Comparing and competing cancels our creativity.

This world is longing for your truth and transparency. When you get clear on who you really are, it may look completely different from the former you, but be assured that it will always be the most attractive version of you! If the real you is quiet, reserved, or perhaps a little shy, don't let someone with a loud, more bold personality make you feel that you are inadequate. Their personality has a place and so does yours. Your persona is needed and was assigned to you for a specific purpose. There are many people in this world who are behind the scenes and still winning. They are not well-known, nor are they a part of any social media platform, yet they are still making big moves and living from a place of peace, joy, and abundance! Popularity does not necessarily equate to living one's truth but living one's truth *does* equate to a purpose-driven life, joyously fulfilled.

Doing what you love is living your truth. No matter what it is, if you love it and it produces good (and no harm) in the world, share it! There is something magical about waking up and finally doing the thing that your heart longs for. I learned this on a greater level on my journey to write this book. What an amazing feeling it is to do something that repeatedly lights my soul. I encourage you to join me on this quest. No matter your background, age, or career, find a way to do what lights you up! Everyone is not meant to be famous, but everyone is meant to bring their special gifts to help transform society for the better. Make your unique, wonderful contribution to this world while you are in human form, and one day when you transition back to spirit, your legacy will beautifully live on.

CHAPTER 29

LOVE IS THE ANSWER

"Keep on, with the force, don't stop 'til you get enough."

—MICHAEL JACKSON

If there is any hate that fills your heart or mind, this is your opportunity to return to love. Why return? Because you were created by love, and when you were born, your innocent heart was filled with love. If you've lost your way, it is time to return now. The love that created you, the love that breathed life into you, the love that allows you to wake each morning, and the love that covers you as you sleep each night awaits your return. It is the love that never dies, the greatest love of all. That love is God.

Ask God to help you with any faults that you have toward another—an individual, group, country, or continent. Be honest. Ask yourself: Why do I have a problem with that person or party? What is being done or said that causes me to feel this way? Are my feelings valid? Did I adopt these feelings from someone else? Is my attitude something that has been handed down to me? Or is it originally my own? What will I gain from hating, hurting, or judging another in this way? By now, you know you will reap whatever it is that you sow. Is it worth spewing out hate or negativity only to receive it back a hundredfold? Absolutely not.

Love is the greatest force on this planet. It has the power to heal all things. When we apply it to ourselves, our relationships, our life purpose, and our world, we will experience miracles! Try it on yourself first. Self-love starts with being grateful for the life you have been given. Accept yourself just as God made you and understand that however you came and in whatever form you were incarnated, it was meant to be. You must not take it for granted. Give thanks. Live your life from a place of gratitude from the moment you wake up each day. If you can speak out of your mouth the words "thank you," God will hear you, and every atom of this universe will respond. The more you give thanks, the more you will have to give thanks for! Love on yourself by edifying God in the body that you have been given. Take care of it. Feed it life-giving foods. Exercise it. Hydrate it well. Give it adequate rest. Be grateful for the vehicle that transports you in this life.

Honor the relationships in your life that serve your highest good and help build you up. Stay clear of those that make you feel low and bring you down. Surround yourself with those who are authentic with good intentions toward you. Be kind and a good friend. Lead with love and it will always find its way back to you.

Do what you love because it is the greatest clue to what your life purpose is. Your work life may not always reflect what you are most passionate about, but if you can find a way to do what lights your soul, a door will inevitably be opened for you.

Love is the antidote for all our suffering. We should allow it to flow through us unconditionally without struggle or strain, without judgment or criticism. Love just because.

CHAPTER 30

A WIN-WIN

"A rising tide lifts all the boats."

—JOHN F. KENNEDY

I n this world, we will have our ups and downs. It comes with the territory. However, when we can fully recognize who we are and the magnificent power that abides within us, then we become unstoppable.

Imagine a world where everyone knew their worth and understood that we came from the source of endless supply. That source intended for us to be here and now. It imparted unique gifts, talents, and skill sets, and is delighted by our use of them. Our very breath is such a privilege! With each inhale and exhale, we are given the glory of God. When we reach the place in which we respect and honor these blessings, we will no longer put energy into ego trips, superficiality, jealousy, competitiveness, or hate. We would walk in full awareness that we all have something wonderful. It's in our DNA and there is no getting around how special we truly are. We would understand that there is enough for everyone, and we can go about the business of becoming our greatest version and living a life of purpose.

If we align our will with the will of the Creator for our lives, we will win. We would never have to wonder if we are on the right path because God's will would be our own. If we come into alignment with that, we can maintain a mindset of peace, joy, kindness, and love. We would think before we act, and our actions would be from a heart of good intentions. Remember that every human carries an energy field (that invisible circle around us). When we set our intentions for positive outcomes, the more positive experiences we will attract to ourselves. If we sow bad seeds, we will reap the same back to us. If we choose war, we will have more of it. If we choose hate, we will have more of it. If we choose *love*, we will always win and have an overflow.

HIGH TIDE

We the people
are riding the waves of life.
We rock high and we dip low.
Hard and heavy the wind blows,
as we wallow back and forth.
Our eyes are blurred by rain and sand.
Fear runs us out of breath,
only to make us gasps for more;
we barely see the shore.
We keep believing, as we are still breathing
and have a chance to survive.
The splash of a hard wave
then suddenly cleanses our eyes.
We can see clearly now.
The tide is now high.
We look around and realize
we are all in the same boat.

CHAPTER 31

WHO IS THE FRIEND WITHIN?

"I'm not a human, I am a dove
I'm your conscience, I am love
All I really need
Is to know that you believe."

—PRINCE, "I WOULD DIE 4 U"

I have cried many times in my life, and in the heaviness of my tears, a sweet, supernatural, reassuring presence reminded me of my worth. It seemed closer than breath, and it welcomed me. It imparted me with power. It seemed to breathe along with me. It soothes my negative thoughts and catches my tears. It seems to stand tall when I need to be affirmed, and it kneels low to pick me up. It calms my racing heart and lets me know that I am loved. It leans in to hear my prayers and gives me strength to keep pursuing my dreams. It responds before I call and gives warning when I enter unsafe territory. It speaks my language and understands me. It gives me signposts and symbols to guide me. It sits with me when I am lonely and reminds me that I am never alone. It blesses me with its energy and helps me to be strong. It blasts me with unexplainable joy when I am hurting and gives peace beyond my understanding. It protects me like a father, and nurtures like a mother. It is a companion like none other.

Its voice is easy and light. When I am doubtful, it gets a little louder. If I am in trouble, an "inner siren" goes off and causes my body to jolt. If I don't know what to ask or pray, an intercession takes over me. It is always accurate and trustworthy. It recharges me with its divine energy. It summons my broken pieces and restores me.

Before I knew it, it knew me. It has journeyed through my life with me. It waits patiently and longs to converse with me. When everyone else left, it has stayed with me.

There is an ever-present force that is with you, greater than any perceived power or authority in this world. It created you, authorized your parents to serve as vessels to bring you, and now and throughout the rest of your life is available to guide and protect you.

I can attest to this power, as the "presence that is never in absence." It is the voice for God. Its power loves and lives with(in) you. It is the spirit of truth. It will be with you. All you must do is call upon it.

To the sweet Holy Spirit, my *friend within*. Thank you for letting me cling to You. You are everything Jesus promised You would be (John 14:15-21)! And so, we continue.

Dear God,
May this message go where You would have it go.
May it be what You would have it be.
May it do what You would have it do.
Thank You for allowing me to be an instrument.
And so it is, Amen.

ACKNOWLEDGMENTS

To my beloved mother, the vessel in which I came: thank you for your demonstration of strength, hard work, dedication, and forever, protective *love*! It is because of you that I learned how to pull myself up and to keep going no matter what. I love you and cherish you in this life, and the life after that, and the life after that.

To Leroy C.G. Wesley II, my high school French and English teacher, a mentor and friend to so many: thank you for being a true egalitarian! Wherever love is, your spirit continues to live.

To Ronny Young, my priceless friend of more than twenty-five years: thank you for standing in the gap, and during my most difficult times, reminding me who I am, where I am from, and what I am made of. Through my mountains and valleys, you stood a solid rock. Eternal love and gratitude to you! You prompted me to one day put it all on paper.

To the earth angels and spiritual guides who have shown up in meaningful and unforgettable ways to support, protect, and encourage me during my moments of deepest despair: Bishop Fred A. Caldwell Sr., Jennie Hawkins-Banks, Eula Segura Pier, Sandra Davis, Patricia Vasquez, Dr. Sharon Judkins, and Dr. Yvonne Lewis. Thank you for demonstrating God's love!

Finally, to Dr. Michael Bernard Beckwith, founder and spiritual director of the Agape International Spiritual Center: your influence and spiritual teachings have helped carve my conscious path. I am grateful for you reflecting the way, teaching the truth, and revealing the life.

ABOUT THE AUTHOR

Monica R. Pierre is a registered nurse who holds a master of science in nursing administration from the University of Texas at Arlington and a bachelor of science in nursing from East Texas Baptist University. She has served in a variety of clinical and managerial roles. Pierre expanded her career as a travel nurse and has cared for patients and clients in a range of settings, from indigent populations to highly affluent residents. She has also earned certifications in holistic health, business, complementary medicine, and spirituality. Her path has allowed her up-close and personal, hands-on education with world-class leaders, offering unconventional wisdom and mentoring. Pierre is a native of Shreveport, Louisiana, and currently resides in the Bay Area of California.

monicapierre.com

Printed in the United States
by Baker & Taylor Publisher Services